KENNEDY GALLERIES, INC.
FOUNDED BY H. WUNDERLICH 1874
THE LIBRARY

KENNEDY GALLERIES, INC.
FOUNDED BY H. WUNDERLICH 1874
THE LIBRARY

EARLY VERMONT WALL PAINTINGS

1790 - 1850

KENNEDY GALLERIES, INC.
FOUNDED BY H. WUNDERLICH 1874
THE LIBRARY

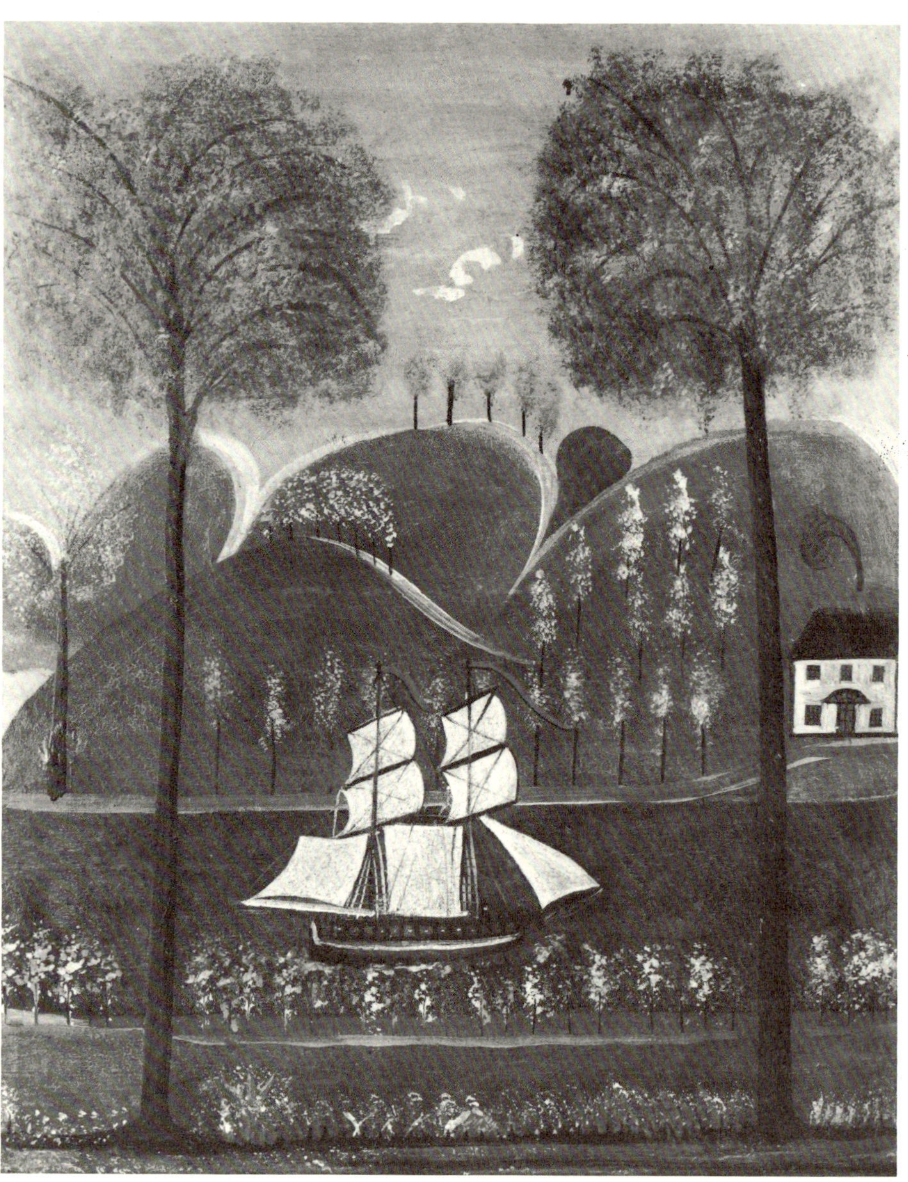

EARLY VERMONT WALL PAINTINGS

1790-1850

BY

Robert L. McGrath

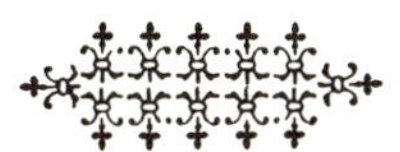

THE UNIVERSITY PRESS OF NEW ENGLAND

HANOVER · NEW HAMPSHIRE

1972

KENNEDY GALLERIES, INC.
FOUNDED BY H. WUNDERLICH 1874
THE LIBRARY

FRONTISPIECE:
"Under Full Sail," see page 47

Copyright © 1972 by Robert L. McGrath
All rights reserved
Library of Congress Catalog Card Number 73-177448
International Standard Book Number 0-87451-062-7
Designed by Klaus Gemming, New Haven, Connecticut
Printed and bound in the United States of America
by Kingsport Press, Inc., Kingsport, Tennessee

*For Robbie, Susie, Felix, Bill
and Vermonters Everywhere*

CONTENTS

ILLUSTRATIONS

ACKNOWLEDGMENTS

THIS BOOK could not have been undertaken without the co-operation of those many obliging Vermonters in whose homes the works of art appear that form the subject of this study. For their patience and hospitality in the face of what must to some have seemed a dubious undertaking, I am deeply thankful. May they find here, in lieu of a list of their names, a further expression of my sincerest gratitude.

I am equally indebted to Nina Fletcher Little, the elegant and gracious *doyenne* of the study of early American wall painting, for many helpful suggestions and criticisms. I am also beholden to Charles Morrissey, Director of the Vermont Historical Society, at whose suggestion this book was written and to Bertram Little and Abbott Cummings of the Society for the Preservation of New England Antiquities for their kindness and encouragement.

Among the many who have contributed to this book I am especially indebted to: Eric de Jonge, Karl Schriftgiesser, Herbert L. Wilson, T. D. Seymour Bassett and Sylvie Pezzoli. My warmest thanks also go to Victor Reynolds for kindly assistance and editorial advice. In addition, my distinguished colleague John Wilmerding deserves much credit for his careful reading of the manuscript and for many insights.

A final note of appreciation is reserved for my friend, companion, and photographer, Edgar Bowen. Whatever small merits this book may possess are primarily due to his skill and energy. I only regret that he did not live to see the finished product of our collaboration.

xiii

INTRODUCTION

THE VIEW that the early settlers of New England were a dour, puritanical lot, given to writing a few crabbed religious verses but otherwise not much taken with the fine arts, is sorely in need of revision. Indeed, I shall always remember my keen sense of astonishment at first entering the old colonial home of a Vermont neighbor and there to be shown, in lieu of the habitual portrait of some stiff ancestor, a series of gay and brightly colored views of valleys, farms, mountains, and seashore painted directly on the white plaster walls. These lively and sensuous decorations were, to be sure, a great surprise and the object of much unanticipated delight, but to my uninitiated eye they would have been more comprehensible on the walls of some Renaissance or baroque palace than in an austere setting of a rural Vermont home. There was, moreover, something oddly disquieting about these rich harmonies of form and color so freely distributed throughout this simple domestic interior. They evoked visions of Renaissance courtiers and worldly prelates rather than Yankee farmers. When it came to the pictorial arts, the latter had always appeared to me like brothers to John Calvin, the ancient Hebrews, or the Byzantine iconophobes. The added disclosure that these paintings were not an aberration—the isolated product of some addled Vermont ancestor of Gulley Jimson—but that wall painting was once a widespread practice throughout much of early New England; came as a revelation as well as a source of lively curiosity.

An attempt to gain additional information on the subject, however, revealed that the study and appreciation of early American wall painting were scarcely beyond the stage of infancy. With the notable exception of a few scholars working alone and mainly self-supported, there was little popular interest in the field, and there was virtually no realization of the material and cultural value of these paintings. Ignorance of this vital and largely unexplored area of early American painting was, I came to discover, ubiquitous. The vitally important questions of care, restoration, and preservation of this heritage had scarcely surfaced, and in this connection the record remains truly dismal.

The study of early American wall painting was initiated by Edward B. Allen's pioneering work *Early American Wall Paintings, 1710–1850* published in 1926. Until the appearance of Nina Fletcher Little's *American Decorative Wall Painting* in 1952, it was the only reference in the field.[1] Mrs. Little's fine book ranks as the most comprehensive study of the subject, though by her own thoughtful admission, it does not represent "a complete or final survey" (e.g., only two of the works dealt with in this book were discussed by her).

More recently, Jean Lipman has written an important monograph that is a model of careful research and sensitive analysis on Rufus Porter, the country's foremost early muralist.[2] With the exception of a few short articles in popular magazines and scholarly journals, however, these works remain the only published studies in a field embracing more than a century and a half of native American folk art. Compared with the deluge of books on minor Renaissance muralists and arcane Pompeian fresco cycles

[1] Edward B. Allen, *Early American Wall Paintings, 1710–1850* (New Haven, 1926); Nina Fletcher Little, *American Decorative Wall Painting, 1700–1850* (New York, 1952).

[2] Jean Lipman, *Rufus Porter, Yankee Pioneer* (New York, 1968).

that appears regularly in this country, the native school of mural decoration receives relatively little attention. Ironically, the frescoes in many of these minor Italian churches or villas—not to mention many of those uncovered by the excavations in Campania, to which we automatically accord full scholarly and critical esteem—are often not superior to those found, as it were, in our own back yard.

This book was undertaken in the belief that the subject of early mural decoration in New England, when studied on a narrow regional basis, would yield more closely defined insights than have been obtained in earlier studies. By widening the frame of reference to include ancient Roman examples of this art form, it is further hoped that a fuller awareness and appreciation of American wall painting and its particular relevance to that earlier society will emerge. At the very least, it offers opportunities for considering these works in a heretofore unexamined light.

My choice of Vermont as the focus of this study is in one sense arbitrary. It was dictated by proximity and sentiment (i.e., I live in Vermont). In a larger and more important sense, however, Vermont offers an ideal field for exploration, if only because previous scholars have tended to concentrate on the murals found in larger neighboring states. Clearly I make no special claims for Vermont murals that do not obtain for those elsewhere in New England. As these states have always shared a form of cultural *lingua franca,* it is certain that the method employed here could be applied elsewhere with equal or better results.

In point of fact Vermont contains fewer examples of early wall painting than New Hampshire, Massachusetts, or Connecticut. Moreover, there are wide disparities in the quality of mural decoration found in the Green Mountain State, ranging from the highest degree of decorative sophistication to works of decided crudeness. Unusual diversity of style, however, compensates for the relative paucity of murals so far discovered in the state. I have yet to encounter wall paintings in two Vermont houses that can be attributed to an identical hand, whereas Rufus Porter is known to have painted in over fifty homes in Massachusetts alone.

As a final note, the notion of comparing the murals of New England with those of Pompeii and Herculaneum is not entirely frivolous. It represents a serious effort to gain new insight into the peculiar sensibilities, both communal and individual, that fostered the growth of mural decoration in the two societies. The approach was suggested not only by similarities of style, medium, and subject—all of which exist but were recognized mainly after the fact—but by my own personal quasi-archaeological experiences in discovering many of the murals. Many were concealed beneath wallpaper or paint and had to be "unearthed" with care. Several had fallen victim to age, fire, or vandalism and required restoration. Rumor, surmise, and luck, always useful companions on a "dig," played a role in bringing to light many of the paintings that are here discussed and reproduced for the first time. And, of course, many treasures still remain hidden beneath ancient strata of paint or paper silently awaiting discovery by some future ardent archaeologist of New England murals.

EARLY VERMONT WALL PAINTINGS
1790 - 1850

CHAPTER I

Pompeii and New England; the Archaeology of Early American Murals

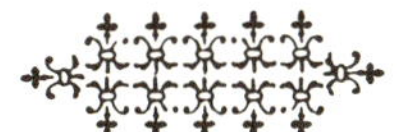

T HE INSTINCT to enlarge and enrich our daily lives with works of art is a universal human phenomenon. Even the most primitive man sought to transform and embellish his environment with painted and sculptural decorations. For many periods of prehistory, art is the major surviving document of a culture or civilization.

In the vital role of enhancing life, the arts and their allied crafts have always been closely associated with the home, whether cave or palace. Yet in the full range of human history only two peoples are known to have applied painted decorations deliberately and consistently to the walls of their ordinary dwellings: the ancient Romans and New Englanders of the eighteenth and nineteenth centuries. Though widely separated by place and time, only these two cultures developed and practiced a widespread and popular mural art, which, insofar as history provides abundant examples, is unique in the art of mankind.

This is not to claim that mural decorations do not occur at other times and places. The history of western art abounds with the names of pharaohs, popes, and princes who have fostered this particular branch of painting. Among the countless wonders of ancient Egypt, medieval Europe, and Renaissance Italy are acres of painted walls and ceilings. These murals, however, appear in temples, churches, and palaces and not in the common dwellings of private individuals. As in all recent societies, mural decoration was a public rather than a domestic art form and, perforce, the spokesman for religious or political institutions rather than for ordinary men.

Admittedly for the two exceptions cited, the average Roman citizen, as well as the New Englander, was often attempting through his use of wall painting to ape the style and accouterments of more patrician ways of life. At base, however, the art brought to the service of these aspirations was popular in nature and often revealed—beneath its pretensions—a thriving democratic spirit. The mural art of the ancient Romans—like that of New Englanders—was in large measure an art of the people, or, as it is commonly called, a folk art.[1] Domestic wall painting therefore belongs generally to that category of nonverbal folklore which survives at a level beneath high or official culture and often provides insights into human nature and society which the more formal aspects of a culture disguise, idealize, or ignore.

In order to achieve meaningful comparisons between Roman and early American mural decoration, one is not obliged to search far beyond the obvious similarity of function to uncover analogous

[1] Amadeo Maiuri, *Roman Painting* (Geneva, 1953), p. 139, notes, for example, that along with "official" Roman painting there was at Pompeii "a whole host of works in which the painter cast off the shackles of tradition and the neoclassical school and set to depicting . . . daily life."

4

features of style, technique, and content. These similarities are moreover hardly a matter of chance. Observers beginning with Jefferson have always had a strong penchant for detecting similar patterns of taste and aspiration within the two societies. As the nearly exclusive domain of the ancient Roman and the early Yankee, domestic wall painting was therefore not surprisingly bent to the service of common human and societal needs.

States dedicated to instilling qualities of independence and self-respect in their citizenry, the republics of ancient Rome and early America appear in history as closely allied in purpose and outlook. "To him," writes an eminent historian of the Roman character, "the knowledge born of experience is worth more than speculative theory. His virtues are honesty and thrift, forethought and patience, work and endurance and courage, self-reliance, simplicity, and humility in the face of what is greater than himself."[2] With a few adjustments to fit the early American point of view, this panegyric may equally describe the reputed qualities of the Yankee.

By way of further analogy, the states of ancient Rome and early America were both societies with a strong basis in rural life. Closely attached to the natural environment, the Roman farmer-citizen, like his Yankee counterpart, was deeply conservative in his outlook on the world. His strong reliance upon nature, however, did not preclude a fundamentally romantic view of it. As a powerful force invested with transcendental values, the natural world provided the material and spiritual focus of his existence. It was at once a reflection of divine law and the proper setting for human enterprise.

[2] Reginald H. Barrows, *The Romans* (London, 1949), p. 11.

Among the more important achievements of the Roman and early American social and political systems was the emergence of numerous individual property owners. Relatively free and self-contained, the citizen-farmer looked to his family (rather than the polis, tribe, or ruler) as the basic sociological unit, with the consequence that private art forms were given unparalleled scope for development. The center for this activity was that unique product of Roman and early American society: the large, single-family home belonging to members of a prosperous rural middle class (i.e., rich farmers).

Taken in combination these factors made possible the rise of art forms independent of the patronage and control of the church and state. Consequently, it is scarcely a matter of chance that many significant points of contact and convergence arise both in form and content in the popular art of Roman antiquity and early republican America.

It is a curious fact that we know more today about the wall paintings of the ancient Romans than about the domestic mural art of early America. Pompeiology, the science and study of the great cycles of wall paintings excavated from the ruins of Pompeii, Stabiae, and Herculaneum, has been an active and distinguished scholarly and critical discipline for well over a century. These vital artistic products of a past civilization, miraculously preserved by the eruption of Vesuvius in A.D. 79, have been the subject of innumerable scholarly monographs as well as a pile of lavish color facsimiles and other forms of coffee-table literature aimed at broad appeal and general consumption. First brought into vogue by the classical revivals of the eighteenth and nineteenth centuries, the mural art of Pompeii still retains a powerful grasp on the scholarly as well as the popular consciousness.

In direct contrast, almost nothing until very recently was known about the wall paintings still to be found in large numbers in the rural colonial houses of New England. The exclusive province of a few scholars and antiquarians, early American wall painting enjoys little of the high standards of care, study, and appreciation given to its ancient counterpart. Even within the broader area of American painting, including the currently fashionable subject of folk art, early mural decoration has received only scant attention.

In view of these circumstance, it comes as no surprise that scholars can inform us more thoroughly about the meaning and purpose of Pompeian frescoes of the first century A.D. than about the much more recent murals of New England. It is far more likely, to cite only one example, that historians are closer to deciphering the enigmatic frescoes in the Villa of the Mysteries at Pompeii than I am to uncovering the historical facts concerning the painting of a strange overmantel in Londonderry, Vermont. (fig. 20)

Similarly, large sums are expended to preserve and restore the painted treasures of Campania while, with few exceptions, little thought or effort is given to safeguarding the murals found in New England homes.[3] At this moment many homes containing wall paintings (which in most other countries would be classified as historic monuments) are neglected and uncared for or, worse yet, have fallen victim to renovation or demolition.

It was this egregious disparity in contemporary attitudes toward Roman and early American wall painting that first suggested the need for a comparative critical approach to these fundamentally kindred art forms. If only a small measure of the justifiable esteem

[3] Jean Lipman, *Rufus Porter, Yankee Pioneer* (New York, 1968), pp. 154–55, reports that the "fate of almost half of the recorded Porter murals" has been papering over, repainting, or outright destruction.

accorded to Pompeian painting could be appropriated for the native school, this study might not appear entirely arbitrary.

At the outset, study of the ancient Roman murals revealed similarities in style, technique, and subject to those of early New England that could scarcely have been anticipated, even by one disposed to distort history to his purposes. To be sure, wall painting in both places was closely associated with daily life and could therefore be expected to provide a reflection of like aspects of these thriving commercial and agrarian societies. Similar views of towns and countryside might also have been foreseen, but not the discovery of nearly parallel representations of such subjects as genre and still life.[4] Further common interests include a surprisingly mutual affection for the polychrome effects of imitation marble,[5] illusionistic architectural perspectives,[6] and an entirely human love of enchanted gardens and fairytale palaces.[7]

[4] Cf. the still life from Herculaneum in the Museo Nazionale at Naples (reproduced in Giulio E. Rizzo, *La Pittura Ellenistico-Romana* [Milan, 1929], pl. CLIII) or one from the house of Julia Felix at Pompeii (reproduced in Maiuri, p. 134) with the painting on wooden paneling from a house in Wallingford, Connecticut (reproduced in Nina F. Little, *American Decorative Wall Painting, 1700–1850* [New York, 1952], fig. 13). In the area of genre, an instructive comparison is provided by the equestrian scene from the house of Julia Felix (Maiuri, p. 139) and an overmantel from the Elisha Hurlbut house in Scotland, Connecticut, attributed to Winthrop Chandler (Little, fig. 53). On the still life in antiquity see Jean-Michel Croisille, *Les natures mortes campaniennes* (Brussels, 1965).

[5] Cf. works of the First or "Incrustation Style" at Pompeii (Maiuri, p. 39) and the examples of "marbleizing" reproduced in Little, figs. 2 and 5.

[6] Cf. the Second Style vista from the Villa of the Mysteries at Pompeii (Maiuri, p. 40) and the deception painting in the Congregational Church at Grafton, Vermont (reproduced in R. L. Towne, "What's Happening in Grafton, Vermont?" *Yankee Magazine,* November, 1967, p. 36).

[7] Cf. Phyllis W. Lehmann, *Roman Wall Painting from Boscoreale in the Metropolitan Museum of Art* (Cambridge, Mass., 1953), for an interpretation of these ancient murals.

In addition to these shared interests, the Roman and the early American wall painter also delighted in the depiction of plant and animal life,[8] scenes of hunting and fishing,[9] and a variety of exotic subjects and events, ranging from tropical landscapes to smoking volcanoes.[10] On occasion, portraits of the owner and his family or relatives appear upon ancient as well as the more recent walls of early New England. (fig. 20) In short, the full scope of human experience together with the real or imagined beauties of the natural world provided the *representata* for these murals.

It may further be argued, both for Roman and American society, that domestic wall paintings served to enlarge the daily lives of average citizens. Not surprisingly, man's natural environment, appropriately embellished by imagination, was among the foremost subjects for artistic concern. Pure landscape, seldom over-burdened with human occupants, freed the imagination in order to permit the spectator to pass from a real to an ideal world within the confines of his own home. In this poetic, beneficent world of nature, it is always summer, midday or twilight, and the sky is never darkened by clouds. (cf. figs. 7 & 8) At times, these bucolic idylls are further enlivened by a roseate sunset.

In these poetic circumstances images tend to arise directly from the artist's imagination, unfettered by the necessity to imitate nature directly.[11] Similarly, when architecture is included, it too

---

[8] For garden scenes see Maiuri, p. 124. Cf. the birds reproduced in Maurizio Borda, *La Pittura Romana* (Milan, 1958), pp. 99, 113, and 120, and the peacocks illustrated in Little, fig. 36.

[9] Among the numerous possibilities here cf. the dog chasing a deer fresco (Borda, p. 114) with the works reproduced in Little, figs. 26 and 28.

[10] Cf. the well-known view of Vesuvius from the house of the Centenario (Rizzo, pl. CXCIX) with the mural reproduced in Little, fig. 141.

[11] Cf. Wilhelmus J. T. Peter, *Landscape in Romano-Campanian Mural Painting* (Assen, The Netherlands, 1963), pp. 193–95.

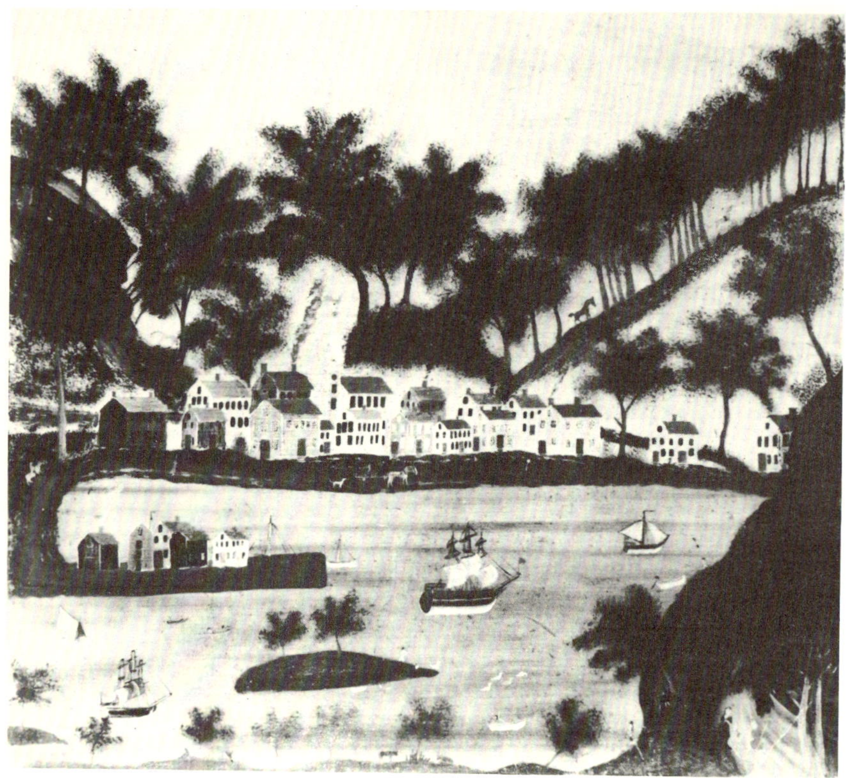

Fig. A: Overmantel from the Tyler-Harrison House, Northfield, Connecticut. Note the amazing similarity of the composition of this painting to the harbor scene from Stabiae (fig. B). In both works a high horizon line is employed to create a vertical perspective which emphasizes the decorated surface rather than spatial or illusionistic values. *Photograph courtesy of Nina Fletcher Little.*

is constructed according to the designs of fantasy. (cf. figs. 5 & 6) By such pictorial means the owner of a rustic country villa could be provided with an endless summer and a luxurious estate far greater than his own. In effect, with the walls of his real environment painted away, a Roman or Yankee farmer possessed a vantage

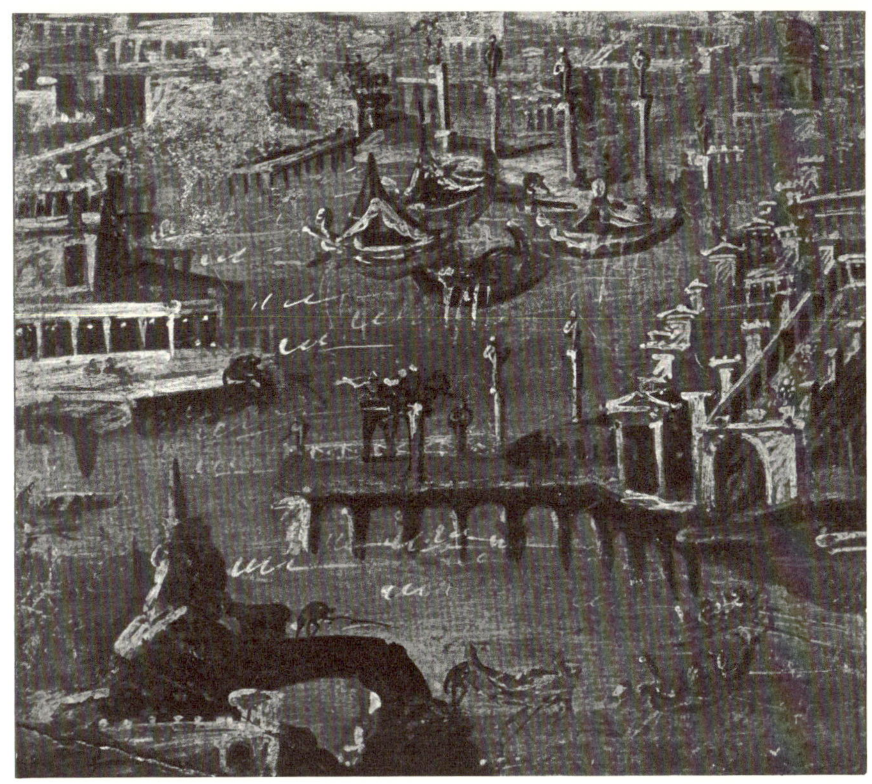

FIG. B: Harbor Scene from Stabiae. *Naples, Museo Nazionale.*

from which he could "survey the ideal property of his dreams."[12]

In these two active maritime societies, views of sea, ship, and harbor also figured prominently on the walls of common dwellings.[13] (Cf. figs. A & B) Through their inherent decorative appeal these scenes also permitted the muralist a degree of independence from the demands for narrative content or topographic accuracy. "Because marine painting was less bound to precedent than other

[12] Lehmann, p. 130.
[13] Maiuri, p. 123, and Little, fig. 46.

genres for subject or manners of painting," John Wilmerding has observed, "it often permitted experimental and fresh expressions."[14]

In this connection still lifes, garden and flower scenes, and the depiction of wild and domestic fauna also provided the Roman and American muralist with the opportunity to investigate formal, as opposed to narrative, problems of art. For these reasons, as well as its popular nature, domestic wall painting was freer and less reliant upon tradition and custom than academic painting. Formal and stylistic innovations, therefore, often occur in murals long before their more noteworthy appearance in official art.

Even the subject of gods, myths, heroes, and sacred rites offers grounds for meaningful comparison with those of New England wall painting, entailing little more than the substitution of Moses or Abraham for Theseus and Zeus.[15] On the whole it is mainly in the realm of erotica that the Yankee muralist sadly fails to provide an equivalency for his Roman counterpart.

One further discerns from a comparative study of ancient and early American mural decoration that foreign influences—after having played a major role in the formation of the respective early styles—gradually gave way to indigenous artistic concerns. This was true equally at Pompeii, where Greek influences and artists were eventually replaced by local Campanian painters, as in early America, where initial European influences were gradually overcome by styles and techniques developed to suit native tastes.[16]

[14] John Wilmerding, *A History of American Marine Painting* (Boston, 1968), p. xii. See also Chapter II for a discussion of the folk art tradition and mural painting.

[15] Cf. Little, fig. 128, and Lipman, figs. 91 and 92.

[16] Maiuri, p. 11.

Historians of Roman painting have been able to discover surprisingly little concerning the ancient muralists. There are only a few names and none are famous. Similarly, the itinerant American limner of the eighteenth and nineteenth centuries retains for the most part his anonymity. As wall paintings were seldom signed, the task of reconstructing individual artistic personalities is much the same for antiquity as for the more recent period. Furthermore, the many bizarre legends connected with the early Yankee muralists are not substantially different from those found in Pliny and other classical sources concerning ancient painters. Invariably set forth as fact, they doubtless tell us more about the way in which the public viewed these bohemians than about the artists themselves.

In the matter of technique, the American wall painter worked in a manner not radically altered from the practice of the ancient muralist. Dry pigments were mixed with glue and water in order to produce the substance known as tempera, which was then applied directly to the dry plaster wall.[17] This fast-drying medium (which is not to be confused with the true *alfresco* technique of the Renaissance muralists) obliged the painter to rely upon directness, simplicity, and sureness of execution. Consequently, in Pompeian as well as in early American murals, artistic effects are mainly derived from pattern and color rather than from draftsmanship. As such, decorative appeal and the overall harmony of the composition invariably take precedence over detailed execution and likeness of persons and places.

In summary, the Roman and early American journeyman painters, despite vast differences in training and background, ap-

[17] *Ibid.,* p. 13.

proached their respective artistic tasks along basically similar lines. Their chief goal was to create the illusion of a three dimensional space on a flat surface and thus permit the enclosed space of the room to merge with that of the external world. On the other hand, these artisan-painters were always mindful of their involvement with the task of architectural decoration and the architectonic, as well as the pictorial, role of murals. Wall decoration was intended to amplify rather than negate the actual structural function of the wall. For this reason, mural decoration was broadly based in both cultures upon an aesthetic of correspondences rather than one of dynamic or calculated imbalances.

There are, to be sure, substantial differences in style and conception between the murals of antiquity and those of early America. Illusionism and plasticity are more important components of Pompeian art than of the native school. As part of the general humanistic ethos of antiquity, the frescoes at Pompeii are more centered on man and his achievements (*megalographia*) than is early American painting, which generally subordinates human to natural values. In terms of style and design, Roman painting advanced "from purely decorative to spatial (i.e., three-dimensional) composition," whereas the development of early American mural decoration runs the reverse course from open-illusionistic vistas to flat, planar, and decorative surfaces.[18] These differences could be multiplied, but in view of the vast geographical and temporal gulf separating these two cultures, they appear far less striking when viewed against the many similarities outlined above.

To some a comparative approach to Roman and American wall painting will doubtless appear forced or specious. The methods of

[18] *Ibid.,* p. 38.

Pompeiology, however, when applied to New England wall painting have yielded several unexpected results. To cite only one useful method gleaned from the study of ancient murals: recent years have seen several attempts to demonstrate that the content of Pompeian wall painting is not made up of a random sampling of pictorial *disjecta membra* but is often the result of deliberate iconographical programs.[19] Phyllis Lehmann, among other leading authorities on Roman painting, maintains that "the walls of Pompeian and Roman houses require interpretation and are not to be brushed aside as a merely decorative assortment of unrelated compositions."[20] It is equally clear that New England wall paintings, in addition to their obvious role as decoration, often possess specific historical and narrative content. Indeed, to dismiss these works as purely ornamental is to fail to apprehend much of their true meaning and to ignore their value as historical and cultural documents.[21] As the student of ancient painting turns to Livy, Strabo, Seneca, or Pliny to gain needed insight, so too must the archaeologist of New England wall paintings resort to the study of records, archives, genealogies, and histories to elucidate their full meaning.

The archaeology of early New England wall painting would also profit from an enlightened awareness of the means employed for the care and preservation of ancient painting. The high standards of technology found in the excavations at Pompeii must replace the "do-it-yourself" mentality that presently characterizes much

[19] See Mary Lee Thompson, "Programmatic Painting in Antiquity," *Marsyas,* X, 1961.

[20] Lehmann, p. 35, fn. 28.

[21] See, for example, Robert L. McGrath, "Rediscovery: Rufus Porter in Vermont," *Art in America,* LVI (January 1968), pp. 78–80.

"restoration" in this country. Directly dependent upon the taste and awareness of private owners, early American wall painting cannot rely upon a catastrophe of Vesuvian proportions to assure its survival for posterity. Meanwhile, the abuse and effacement of this artistic patrimony show little sign of abating.

As monuments of great aesthetic value and documents of cultural and historical significance, early American wall paintings offer a unique pictorial record of a major period of our early history. It is hoped that these remarks will contribute to the recognition of these facts, as well as provide tentative outlines of a comparative methodology for their study and wider appreciation.

Painting on Overmantels

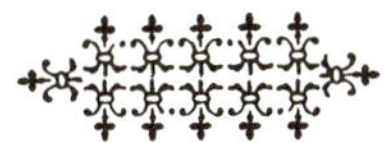

Vermont has been called the child of Connecticut, a relationship that holds true in the cultural as well as the more obvious social and demographic sense. Not only did the Green Mountain State's first farmers, tradesmen, and politicians come from Connecticut, but for all the reputed austerity of these early settlers, the artists also soon followed the route of migration northward along the Connecticut River Valley.

Early Vermont homes, for example, offer testimony to these connections in often following patterns of construction and design that originated with Connecticut builders.[1] Similarly, the earliest examples of decorative wall painting found in Vermont houses display close stylistic affinities with works that first appeared in Connecticut. Usually the product of itinerant limners plying their trade along the paths of settlement, decorative wall painting was closely allied to early domestic architecture in Vermont. In some

[1] See Philip A. White and Dana D. Johnson, *Early Houses of Norwich, Vermont* (Hanover, N.H., 1938), pp. 11–17 for a discussion of Connecticut influences on Vermont domestic architecture.

instances painting was actually practiced by carpenters or wood-workers in addition to their regular skills.

The earliest forms of decorative wall painting found in Vermont, as elsewhere in New England, are pictures designed for overmantel boards situated on the chimney breast above fireplaces. This form of painting, as Nina Fletcher Little has shown, was introduced into the colonies during the second quarter of the eighteenth century from England where it was much in vogue.[2] In no case, however, should painted chimneypieces be confused with framed pictures intended to be hung on the wall. In the first place the function of a chimneypiece is determined by the architectural setting from which it has no structural or formal autonomy. As part of the permanent structure, the overmantel board therefore requires integration with the larger ornamental scheme of the room.

Though the painter's goal was to dissolve pictorially a section of the wall by means of illusion, he was also responsive to the architectonic role of the work. Consequently, compositions for overmantel paintings tend to be balanced, frontal, and planar. Diagonal recessions and asymmetrical schemes (despite their popularity in conventional easel painting) are seldom employed, mainly in the interest of preserving the compositional stability and decorative harmony of the pictorial and architectural ensemble. Any tension arising from the space of the picture and the closed, finite dimensions of the room usually finds resolution in the elaborate paneling and moldings. These provide a kind of transition from an open three-dimensional world to the flat, planimetric surface of the

[2] Nina F. Little, *American Decorative Wall Painting, 1700–1850* (New York, 1952), p. 17.

walls. Thus a gradual merger is achieved between the world of illusion provided by the picture and the reality which is one's own room.

Though the earliest overmantel panels in the colonies were the work of transplanted Europeans, by the time of the Revolution, artists in Massachusetts and Connecticut had begun to develop an indigenous style based on the rural New England countryside. The earliest overmantels generally featured simplified views of landscape, though in a few instances where European prints or paintings were employed as a basis for composition (Cf. figs. 10 & 11), native artists thoroughly Americanized their sources.[3]

For the most part the early American landscape style that appears in the overmantels differs from its European counterpart by virtue of a total absence of romanticizing overtones. Instead, there is a more direct approach to the reality of nature, although these works are generally products of imagination rather than observation.

1 · The Partridge-Snell House

No wall painting in Vermont can safely be dated prior to the last decade of the eighteenth century. The date of the earliest known example of overmantel painting in the state corresponds roughly with Vermont's reluctant acquisition of statehood in 1791. It is found in the Partridge-Snell house in the town of Norwich, one of the earliest sites of settlement in the upper Con-

[3] See Little, p. 36 and figs. 34 and 35, for an early Massachusetts overmantel and an English print that served as its source.

necticut River Valley. Among the foremost surviving examples of
the colonial style in early Norwich, the Partridge-Snell house was
built one year after the start of the Revolution. The original
owner was Elisha Partridge who had come to Norwich from Connecticut with his parents in 1765.[4] He was later commissioned a
lieutenant and fought together with his three brothers in the war
for independence.[5]

Recently discovered in one of the upstairs bedrooms beneath
several layers of white paint is a large (41″ x 51″) overmantel
(fig. 1) painted in oil on two expertly joined wooden panels. The
principal decoration of the panel consists of four trees silhouetted

[4] On the early history of Norwich see Merritt E. Goddard and Henry V.
Partridge, *A History of Norwich, Vermont* (Hanover, N.H., 1905). See also
White and Johnson, p. 20 and fig. 23, for the Partridge-Snell house.

[5] See Goddard and Partridge, pp. 231–32 for the history of the Partridge
family.

Fig. 1: Overmantel in the Partridge-Snell House, Norwich, Vermont.

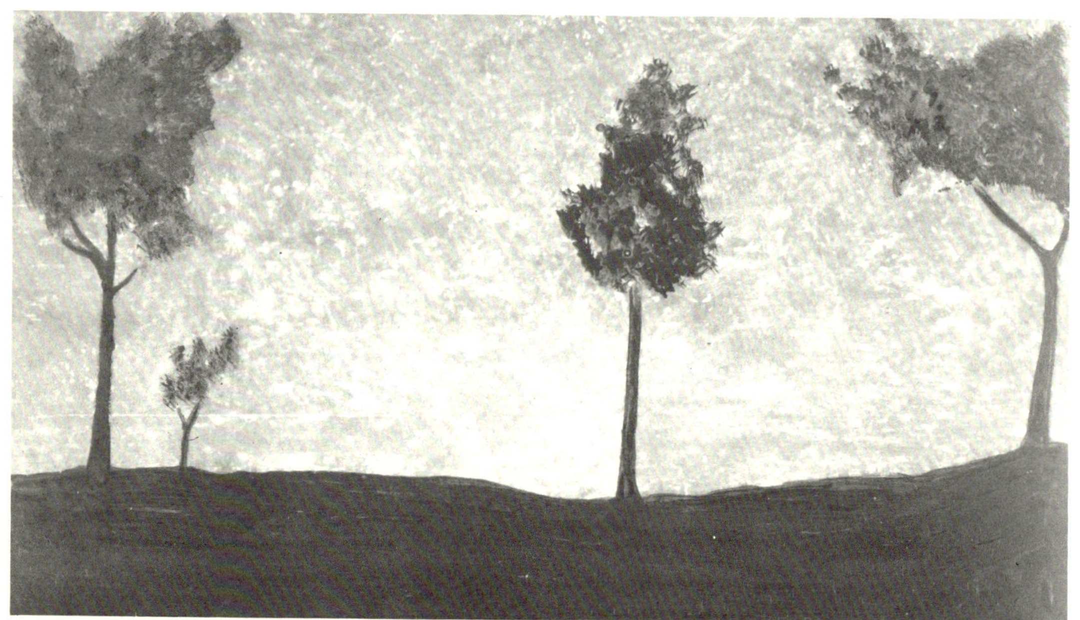

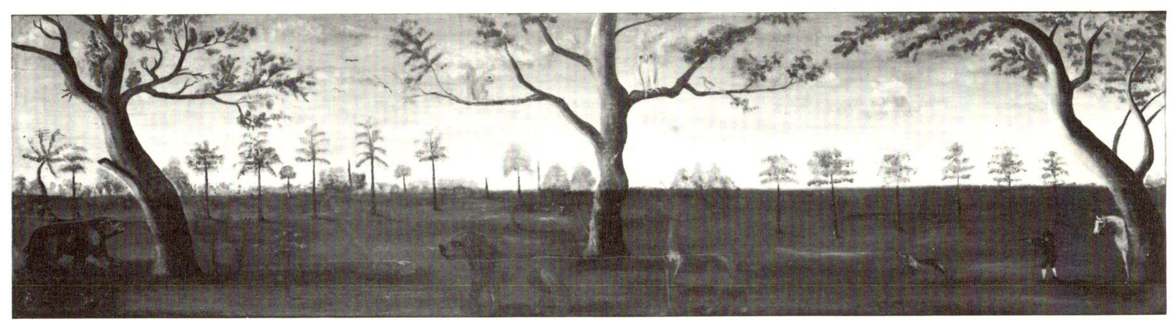

FIG. 2: Overmantel from the Coles-Searle Tavern, Brooklyn, Connecticut.
The Metropolitan Museum of Art, Lee Fund, 1937.

starkly against a dull gray green background. A softly undulating ground plane is elevated to about midpoint on the picture surface, thereby creating a high, characteristically primitive horizon line. At the right a large elm has been truncated (both literally and figuratively) to suggest the extension of space beyond the carved frame molding. This latter is an especially sophisticated device for the provincial artisan who executed the otherwise simple work.

Another unusual feature of the Norwich panel, apart from its ruthless austerity, is the complete absence of animal or human occupants in the scene. Despite the temptation to view this as a deliberate evocation of a wilderness hostile to mankind, it is probably attributable to the artist's inexperience and the problems of *staffage* (accessory human or animal figures) common to many early American landscape paintings.

As previously suggested, the likely model for this frugal composition is found in a group of Connecticut overmantels dating from the 1770s and 1780s of which the Norwich panel is a simplified version. A hunting scene from the Coles-Searle tavern in Brooklyn, Connecticut (presently in the New York Metropolitan Museum of Art—fig. 2), for example, displays a similar grouping of trees, large and small, lined up against the horizon like so many sentinels at attention. As in the Norwich panel, the elm at the right has been cut off arbitrarily by the frame of the picture.[6] In like manner, a high ground line divides the Connecticut overmantel horizontally into roughly two equal parts, while a simple staccato rhythm is formed by the verticals of the trees. By contrast, the Connecticut scene is enriched by the presence of a diminutive hunter and several delightful animals, suggesting that the original source for the work may have been an English sporting print.

Although it has since been destroyed by fire, another Connecticut panel by the same painter is illustrated in E. B. Allen's *Early American Wall Paintings* and provides additional close analogies in style and compositional scheme to the Norwich overmantel.[7] The description of the predominant hues, greens and reddish browns, in this panel further confirms the stylistic proximity of the two works.

On the strength of these comparisons, there need be little hesitation in attributing the Norwich panel to a Connecticut trained artist active in Vermont toward the close of the eighteenth century. Responsive to the stern Vermont environment, he provided a totally unidealized record of it which, in its starkness and austerity, is not without charm to the modern eye accustomed to the sophisticated economies of a Cézanne landscape or a Braque still life.

[6] For the Brooklyn overmantel see Edward B. Allen, *Early American Wall Paintings, 1710–1850* (New Haven, 1926), p. 16 and fig. 14, and Little, p. 53 and fig. 52.

[7] See Allen, p. 15 and fig. 13.

A second painted overmantel (fig. 3) executed in the closing years of the eighteenth century is found in the northwest parlor of an elegant brick house located near Jericho in the Winooski valley.[8] Built as a wedding gift for his son Martin by Vermont's first governor Thomas Chittenden, the house was probably completed in 1796, one year before the governor's death. Much of the evidence for this dating is suggested by the overmantel (50″ x 39″) which, according to legend, was painted by one of the workmen on the home named Sprague.[9] Among the objects represented on the panel are the Federal eagle, a liberty cap, and the American flag containing sixteen stars. Other patriotic symbols include a cow and three sheaves of wheat, both of which still appear in the Vermont state seal. Additional local significance appears in an outsized spruce and a conventionalized view of the Green Mountains.

Though the number of stars found on a flag is, in the opinion of Nina Fletcher Little, "a notably unreliable indication of date," in this case it probably has some basis in historical fact.[10] As Tennessee was the sixteenth state admitted to the union in 1796 and Governor Chittenden died in 1797, the former date appears relatively secure for the work.

Overmantels decorated with patriotic symbols are not uncom-

[8] See Herbert W. Congdon, *Old Vermont Houses* (New York, 1946), pp. 67–68.

[9] *Ibid.*, p. 67. The overmantel was formerly covered by a vapid late nineteenth century painting on canvas that is reproduced in the first edition of Congdon's book (Brattleboro, Vt., 1940), p. 20 and fig. 4, as the work of Sprague. Fortunately the painting on canvas was removed and the error rectified in the second edition of the book.

[10] Little, p. 49.

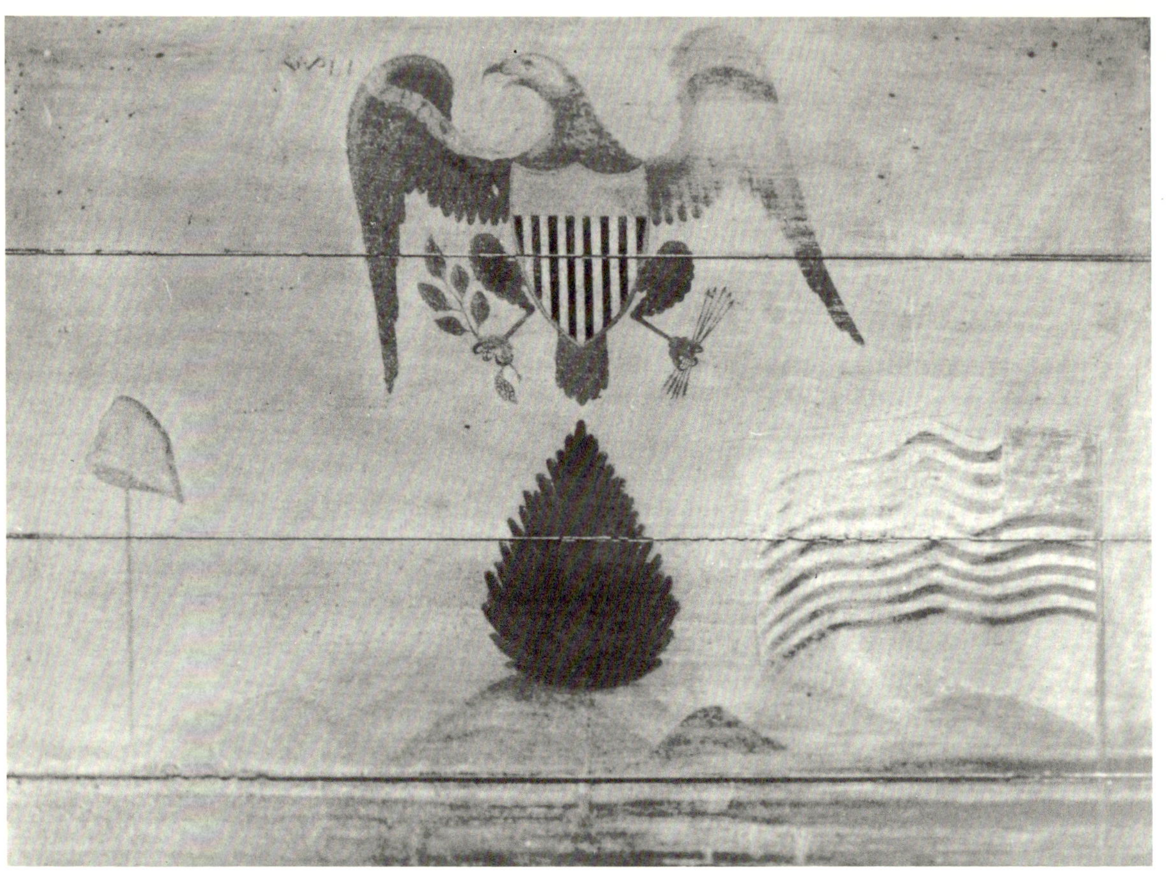

FIG. 3: Overmantel in the Chittenden-Martin House, Jericho, Vermont.
*Photograph courtesy of the Herbert W. Congdon Collection, Bailey Library,
University of Vermont.*

mon in New England, eagles having been found in houses in
Duxbury, Massachusetts, and in Exeter and Henniker, New
Hampshire.[11] The recent discovery in a house in southeastern

[11] *Ibid.,* figs. 50 and 132. For a reproduction of the Henniker panel see John M.
Howells, *The Architectural Heritage of the Merrimack* (New York, 1941), fig.
302.

24

Pennsylvania of a magnificient nine-by-sixteen-foot mural on plaster of the eagle and the flag set in a mountainous landscape (fig. 4) also indicates that the appeal of these subjects was fairly widespread throughout the early Republic. Painted about 1850 by an immigrant of Swiss or German ancestry who sometimes signed his work with the name Louis Mader, this painting is one of an extremely rare group of early mural decorations found outside of New England.[12] Together with the overmantel from the Chittenden house, the Mader mural is one of the finest examples of this particular genre of patriotic painting in early America.

Of particular interest in connection with the overmantel in the Chittenden house is the beautifully carved woodwork that decorates the chimney breast. Probably no finer example of a rope-carved molding exists in an old Vermont home. Handsomely gilded, this elaborate device promotes a keen decorative harmony between the painting and its architectural setting.

[12] See the Lancaster, Pennsylvania, *New Era,* July 31, 1965.

FIG. 4: Patriotic mural in the Cochran House, Quarryville, Pennsylvania, attributed to Louis Mader. *Photograph courtesy of the William Penn Memorial Museum, Harrisburg, Pennsylvania.*

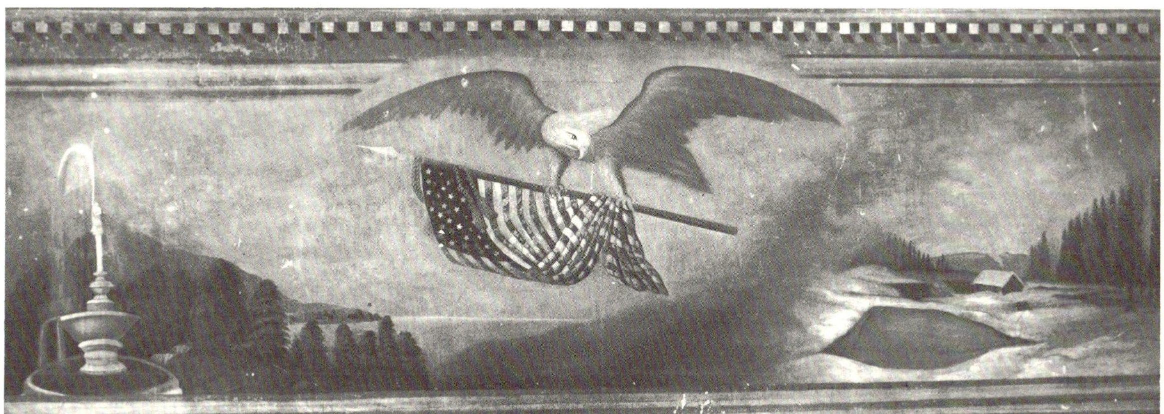

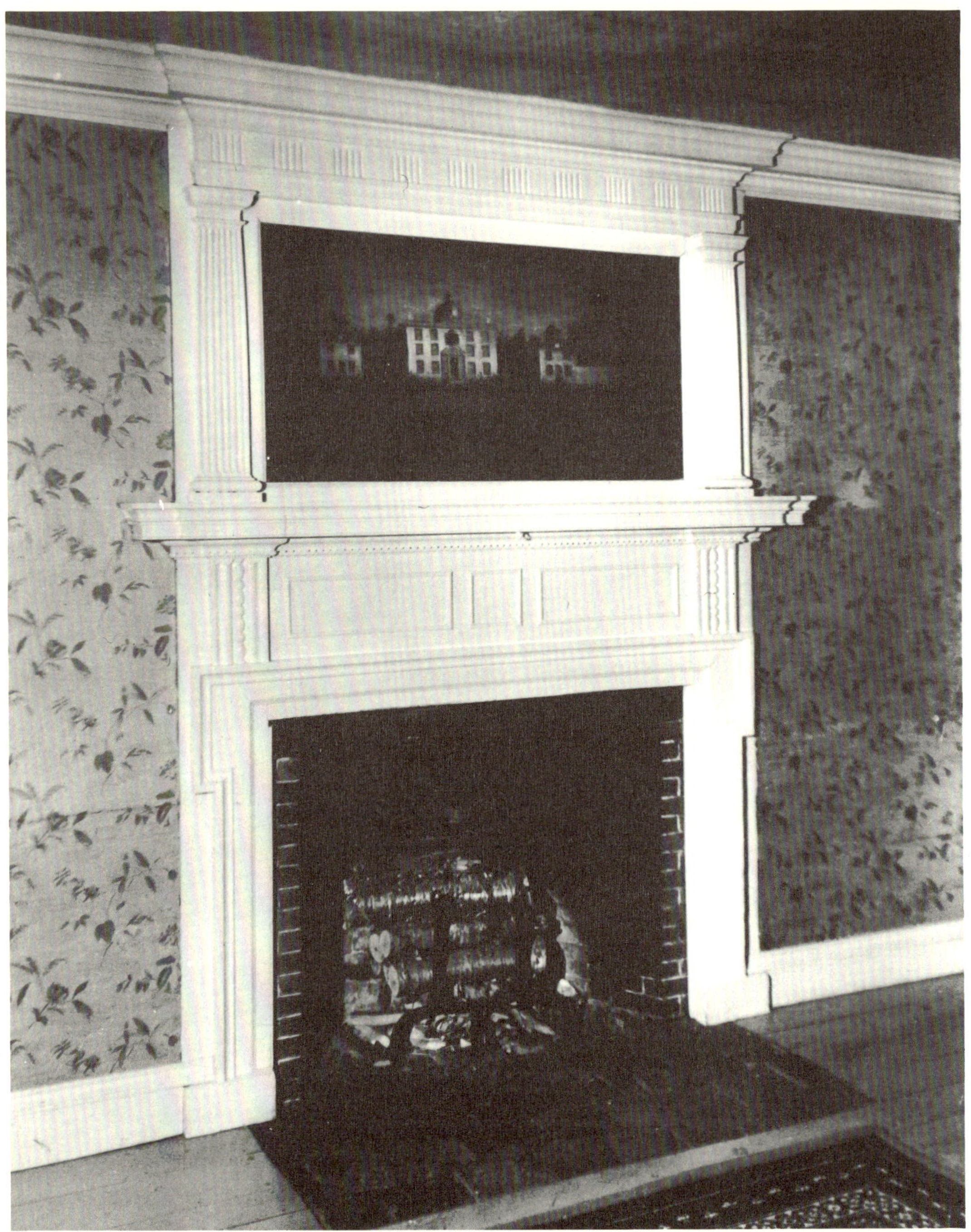

FIG. 5A: Overmantel in the Old Rich Tavern, North Montpelier, Vermont.

In 1805 Samuel Rich built a home for himself and his family which, then as now, was one of the finest examples of Georgian architecture anywhere in Vermont.[13] The lumber for his new house came from Mr. Rich's sawmill and the bricks from his own brickyard. So prosperous, indeed, did he become that the small community in which the Rich mansion stood came to be known as Rich's Hollow, but the modern visitor is better advised to seek North Montpelier.

According to the present owners of the house, the master carpenter was one William Isaac Wells, "Old Isaac," who had twenty-two children by two wives. The identity of the artist, however, who painted the unusual overmantel (figs. 5a and 5b) in the ladies' parlor is a total mystery. No one knows his name, nor is it certain when the work was done.

Enframed by a superb Doric molding, the panel depicts a large and important estate. The principal building in the picture is a three-story structure containing a prominent elliptical doorway above which is situated a handsome Palladian window. An elegant freestanding balustrade accentuates the flat roofline. Small two-story flanking dependencies appear at either side of the central building and indicate the height of a wall surrounding the entire estate. In the interstices between the smaller structures and the main house, one catches sight of well-tended fields and distant lines of trees. Finally, the main house is imperiously crowned by a great golden dome whose lines are repeated in the graceful arc of

[13] See Harold Child, *Gazetteer of Washington County, Vermont* (Syracuse, N.Y., 1889), p. 267 for the history of Samuel Rich and his family.

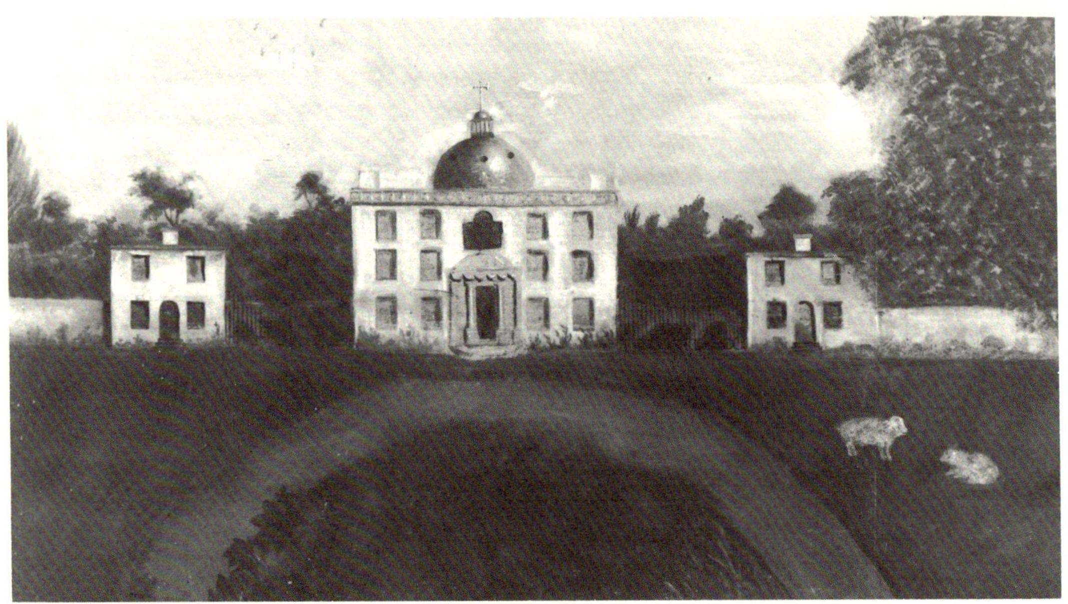

Fig. 5b: Closeup of overmantel in the Old Rich Tavern, North Montpelier, Vermont. This fanciful vision of a dream villa should be compared with the wall painting from an ancient villa at Boscoreale (fig. 6) where a similar attempt was made to evoke illusions of grandeur.

the driveway that leads the viewer's eye up to the estate. Beneath the customary elm at the lower right of the picture, a herd of grazing sheep provides a curious contrast to the total absence of human occupants in these luxuriant surroundings.

No modern visitor to Samuel Rich's house is likely to mistake it for the palatial edifice represented in the parlor overmantel. For all of its Georgian finery, the Rich house is a poor and distant cousin of the Federally inspired mansion depicted in the painting. Indeed, it is unlikely that any such estate ever existed in early nineteenth-century New England outside of the imagination of

28

the artist and his patron.[14] On the contrary, the massing of the buildings (especially the use of flanking dependencies) evokes visions of lush Southern plantations rather than Yankee architecture of the period.[15]

Closer to home, a partial source for Samuel Rich's magnificent villa can be found in the designs of the great architect of the

[14] Little, p. 20, "seldom does the mansion in an overmantel panel prove to be the house from which the painting actually came."

[15] E.g., Thornton's Tudor Place near Washington. See A. Peter, *Tudor Place Designed by Dr. William Thornton* (Georgetown, 1969). For a discussion of the plantation style see Henry R. Hitchcock, *Architecture, Nineteenth and Twentieth Centuries* (Baltimore, 1958), pp. 82–84.

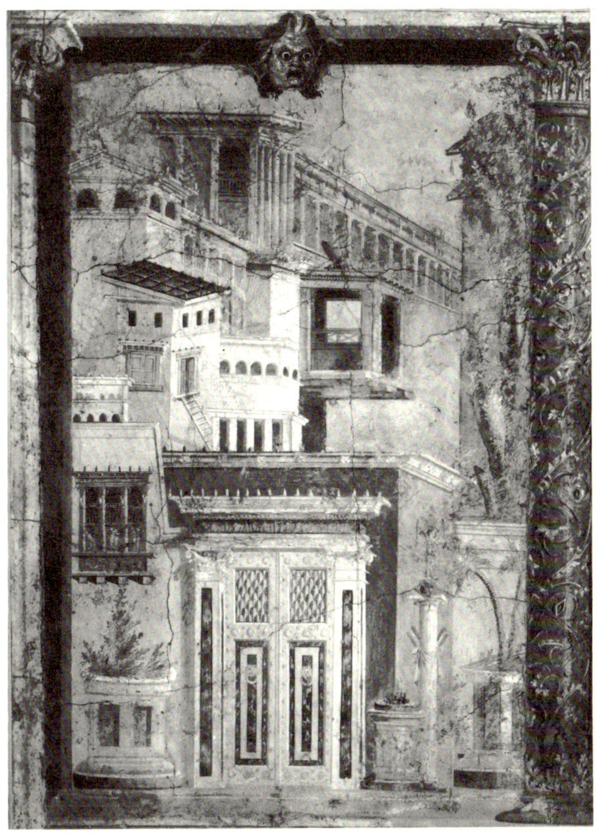

FIG. 6:
Mural from a villa at Boscoreale.
*The Metropolitan Museum of Art,
Rogers Fund, 1903.*

Federal style Charles Bulfinch of Boston (1763–1844). In attempting to conceive of an ideal country property, the artist seems deliberately to have grafted the best features of Bulfinch's public and domestic architecture onto rudiments of the Southern plantation style. Thus, for the main building he might have employed the design of the first Harrison Grey Otis house (1796) and capped it with the golden dome of the Boston State House (1795–98).[16]

Engravings of Bulfinch's designs appearing in newspapers or magazines of the time probably served as models for the painter. In addition, his awareness of current architectural styles stands in direct contrast to the provincial designer of the Rich mansion, who as late as 1805 was still building in the Georgian style. As the date of the old Rich mansion falls roughly midway in the *floruit* of the Federal style in America (1790–1820), there is no compelling reason to assign a later one to the painting. In this instance, at least, the overmantel may well be contemporary with the house in which it occurs.

The notion of having an estate that is greater than one's own property painted in a private home bears strong resemblance to a previously mentioned practice in Roman painting. As Phyllis Lehmann has shown, the frescoes from the Boscoreale cubiculum (fig. 6) representing luxurious architectural fantasies probably served the function of enabling the owner to escape from his mundane existence to a world of make-believe.[17] The fairytale

[16] See Richard McLanathan, *The American Tradition in the Arts* (New York, 1968), p. 138, for reproductions of these Bulfinch designs.

[17] Phyllis Lehmann, *Roman Wall Paintings from Boscoreale in the Metropolitan Museum of Art* (Cambridge, Mass., 1953), p. 130.

estate depicted in Samuel Rich's house no doubt served a similar purpose in enabling that prosperous tradesman to extend his ego far beyond the rural Vermont community in which he lived into the opulent life-style depicted on the wall of his home.

4 · The Murdock-Pierce House

Located slightly north of Norwich is an elegant country home in the Georgian style that is unrivaled anywhere in town for its architectural sophistication. It was built *circa* 1788 by Constant Murdock (1761–1828), a younger son of one of the wealthiest and most prominent Norwich families, to house his new wife, Sarah Jewett.[18] The paintings, following the scheme of the earlier Partridge-Snell house in Norwich, are found above fireplaces in the upstairs bedrooms. They are, however, the work of a different artist and slightly later in date.

The overmantel panel in the southwest bedroom (fig. 7) is of special interest because of its unusual subject and the high quality of its execution. The main feature of the overmantel (33″ x 39″) is a handsome country estate that is surrounded by high fences and flanked by avenues of trees. At the right of the panel and situated in the middle distance is a smaller house that fronts on a pond sufficiently large to contain a sailboat and its diminutive occupant.

Though sadly disfigured by a hole cut to accommodate the later addition of a stovepipe, the painting still retains much of its original appeal and decorative charm. The colors are lively and

[18] White and Johnson, p. 23.

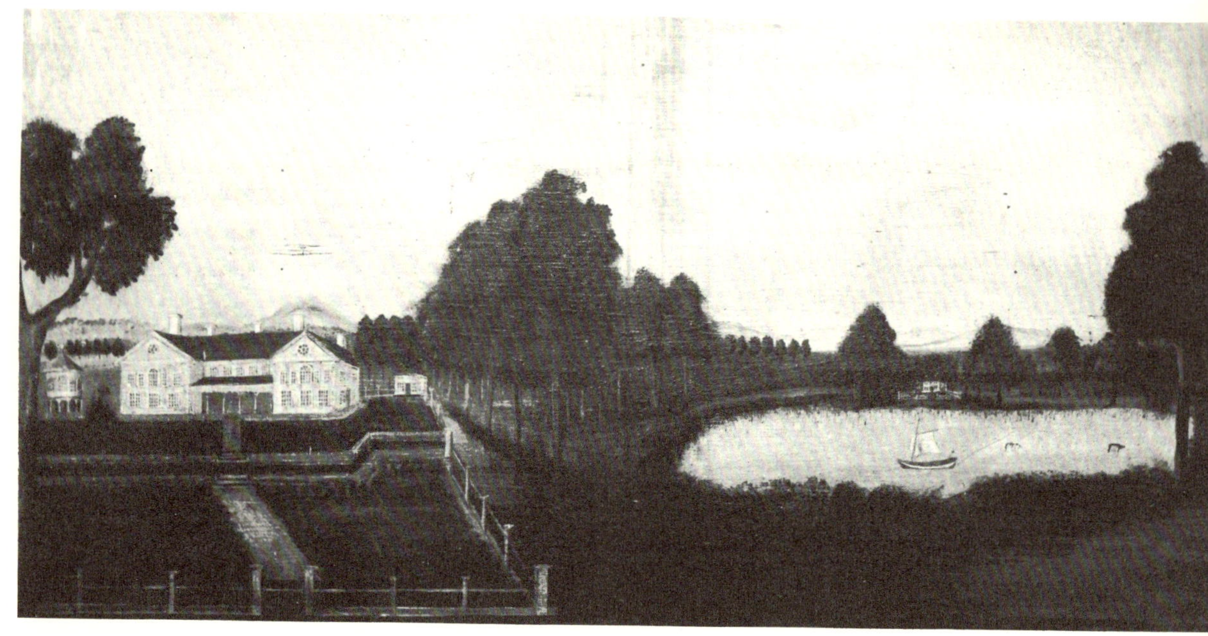

FIG. 7: Overmantel in the Murdock-Pierce House, Norwich, Vermont. This idyllic landscape vista can be compared favorably with a mural from Pompeii (fig. 8) where a similar pavillioned villa also appears. Note in addition the presence of a small sailing vessel at the lower right of each composition.

naturalistic with greens and browns attractively set off against a rosy sunset sky. A characteristically primitive touch is provided by the tilted foreground perspective which combines with the low horizon line to create an unusually bold recessional effect.

The principal building depicted in the panel is a large colonial mansion composed of an open arcaded main body and two projecting wings. Additional buildings include a small barn or a stable and what appears to be a round gazebo or garden pavilion perched upon a circular arcade.

Is this grandiose spectacle (like Samuel Rich's overmantel)

another attempt to gratify the aspirations and fantasies of some
pretentious rustic, a kind of pictorial wish fulfillment? Normally
one might be inclined to view it in this light but for the discovery
of evidence that opens up another possible interpretation. In the
History of Norwich is found a description of a large estate that
once existed in town that provokes comparison with several details represented in the overmantel. According to this account,
Jasper Murdock (1759–1803), the older brother of Constant,
built a remarkable house in Norwich in the 1780s which, until
its destruction by fire in December of 1889, was said to have been
"one of the finest at that time in the state."[19] The description

[19] Goddard and Partridge, p. 227.

Fig. 8: "Villa Rustica" from Pompeii. *Naples, Museo Nazionale.*

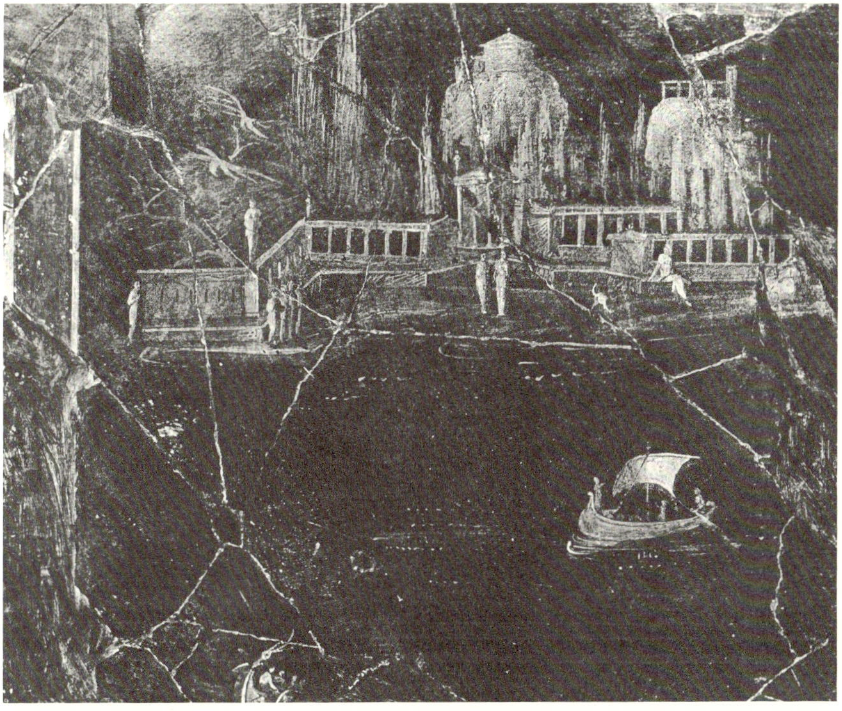

further indicates that the main body of the house was *"flanked by two wings, each large enough for a private residence."* (author's italics) The grounds, it seems, were especially lovely, containing a large flower garden and an impressive fish pond. In view of the close correspondences between the written description and the scene depicted in the overmantel, there is a strong possibility (for all the Freudian implications of the conclusion) that the work is a portrait of Jasper Murdock's fine estate.

As neither photographs nor engravings of the house survive, it is far more likely, however, that the artist drew upon architectural formulas, symbolic of the good life in an ideal world, to create this scenic idyll.[20] In the final analysis both of the above interpretations are admissible, for at least one Baltimore painter advertised in 1792 that he could do "Landscapes either from Nature or Fancy."[21]

In the northwest bedroom is found a second and considerably larger (42″ x 64″) painting (fig. 9). The viewer, however, is confronted by a new medium because the work is no longer painted on a wooden panel but directly on the plaster wall. In imitation of a wooden overmantel, the painting is located over the fireplace and is framed by elaborate wooden paneling. An added effect is created by a band of greenish gray painting simulating marble that runs across the wall above the scenic mural and thereby form-

[20] Cf. Allen, fig. 15, for a Connecticut panel showing a large house with similar projecting wings. Such popular builders' guides as William Pain's *The Practical House Carpenter* (London, 1815), pl. 109, or John Crunden's *Convenient and Ornamental Architecture* (London, 1791), pls. 20, 24, and 31, also contain numerous engravings of ideal country estates which may have provided source material for the painter.

[21] Little, p. 23.

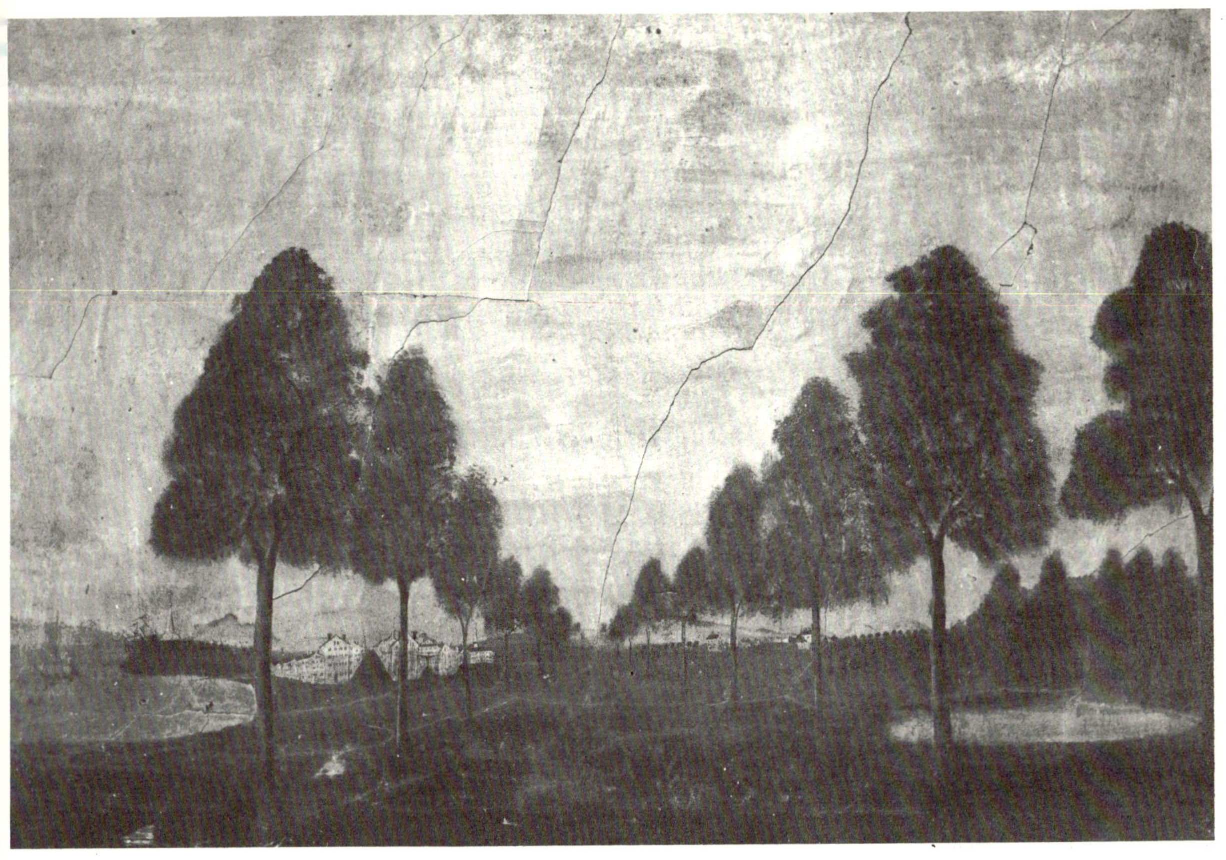

FIG. 9: Overmantel on plaster in the Murdock-Pierce House, Norwich, Vermont.

ing a transition from the world of pictorial illusion to that of architectural reality.[22] This technique of "marbleizing" is frequently encountered in other New England states but is known in Vermont only from this single surviving example. Finally, in

[22] *Ibid.,* pp. 6–12, for a discussion of the techniques of "marbleizing" and other forms of early architectural decoration.

order to separate the picture surface from the areas of simulated marble as well as the actual wooden paneling, there is a painted margin of black which serves as a frame.

The entire painted ensemble, frame, scenic mural, and ersatz marble, was executed in the unusual technique of oil on dry plaster. Despite the fact that advertisements appear in early newspapers announcing such skills as the painting of "rooms in oil or water in a new taste," no previous house has been discovered anywhere in early America in which the technique of oil on plaster was actually employed for scenic purposes.[23] The far more usual practice, as previously noted, was to paint with a mixture of glue, water, and dry pigments which in the early accounts is called "distemper."[24]

Not only is the Norwich painting a unique example of mural technique but, more important, it indicates the initial reliance of early wall decoration on overmantel painting. This form of decoration further appears to have begun as a cheap and convenient substitute for overmantel painting. In fact, the artist of the mural is certainly identical with the painter of the wooden overmantel in the southwest bedroom. Among numerous common conventions, he employs, for example, a low horizon line similar to that seen in the overmantel, and an identical color scheme, among other analogous features of style, is found in both works. The arrangement of trees in artificial rows to create perspective recessions occurs in both paintings as does an equivalent disposition of ponds, lakes, mountains, and elements of architecture.

Depicted at the left of the picture is a kind of urban seaport, the

[23] *Ibid.,* pp. 80–82.
[24] For a recipe see Little, p. 81.

first appearance of a marine subject in a Vermont home. As such views are not indigenous to Vermont, conventional formulas doubtless provided the basis for such decoration. Rows of town houses and sailing ships, one of which is docked before a curious domical structure, form the major content of the work. The most conspicuous feature of the painting, however, is an avenue of large trees which creates a dynamic recession and leads the spectator's eye from the foreground to the middle distance at virtually break-neck speed.

Another overmantel panel (fig. 10) recently taken from a home in Cornish, New Hampshire, can also be attributed to this unknown artist. Presently in a private collection, this charming rural scene provides a useful comparison with the Norwich paintings. It further reveals the likely source for many of these early overmantels which, taken as a group, constitute some of the first pure landscapes in American painting, antedating by almost half a century the better known Hudson River school.[25]

Engravings from abroad or from local newspapers and magazines provided a source for many of these early New England overmantels, as Nina Fletcher Little has observed.[26] English mezzotints and engravings were especially popular as a source for landscape schemes, wherein the Thames could be transformed into the Connecticut (Cf. figs. 10 and 11) or some other New England river.[27]

[25] See Abbott L. Cummings, "The Beginnings of American Landscape Painting," *The Metropolitan Museum of Art Bulletin,* XI (1952), pp. 93–98.

[26] Little, pp. 34–36.

[27] See also the article by Nina F. Little, "English Engravings as Sources of New England Decoration," in *Old Time New England,* LIX (1964), pp. 96–102.

Additional inspiration for these scenic overmantels is found in the landscape schemes developed to serve as background for a number of late eighteenth-century American portraits. The overmantel from Cornish, for example, bears a striking resemblance to the landscape background in Ralph Earl's portrait of Major Daniel Boardman of 1789 in the National Gallery (fig. 12) ; witness the placement of trees and shrubbery, the characteristic bend of the river, the houses with prominent fences supported on high

FIG. 10: Overmantel from the John Mason House, Cornish, New Hampshire. *Photograph courtesy of Nina Fletcher Little.*

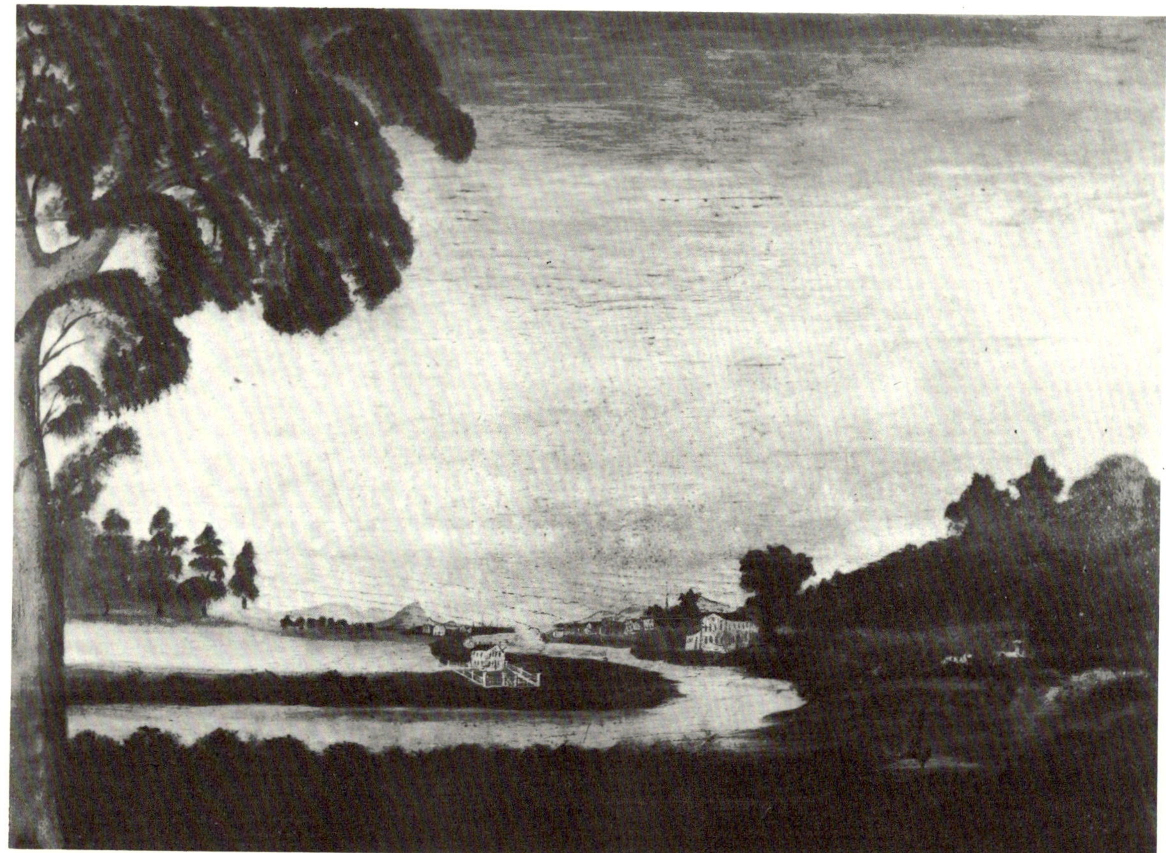

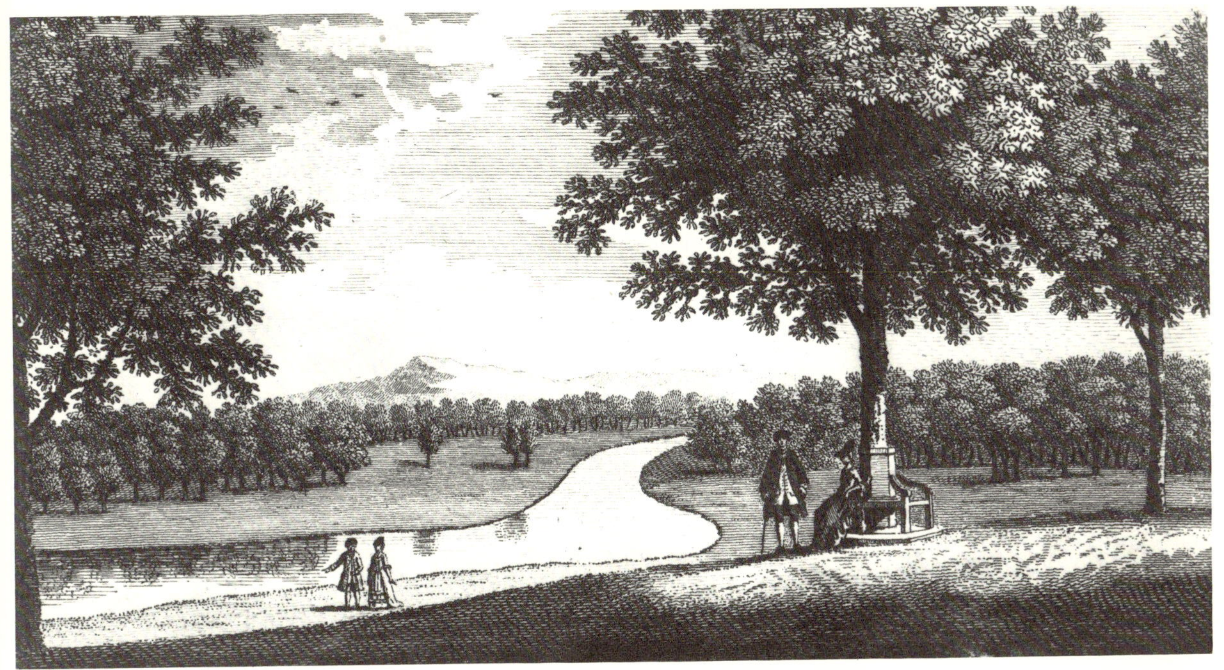

FIG. 11: "View from the Terrace at Oat-lands" from: *A New Display of the Beauties of England*, London, 1776. *Photograph: Society for the Preservation of New England Antiquities.*

posts, et cetera.[28] Similarly, the mural in the Murdock-Pierce house compares favorably with the window view in Joseph Steward's fine portrait of John Phillips in the Dartmouth College collection (fig. 13). One notes in both works the formal arrangement of tree-lined avenues employed for perspective purposes together with an awareness of atmosphere as a further means of achieving pictorial space.

[28] On Ralph Earl, who is considered "the pioneer American landscapist," see Lawrence B. Goodrich, *Ralph Earl* (Albany, N.Y., 1967).

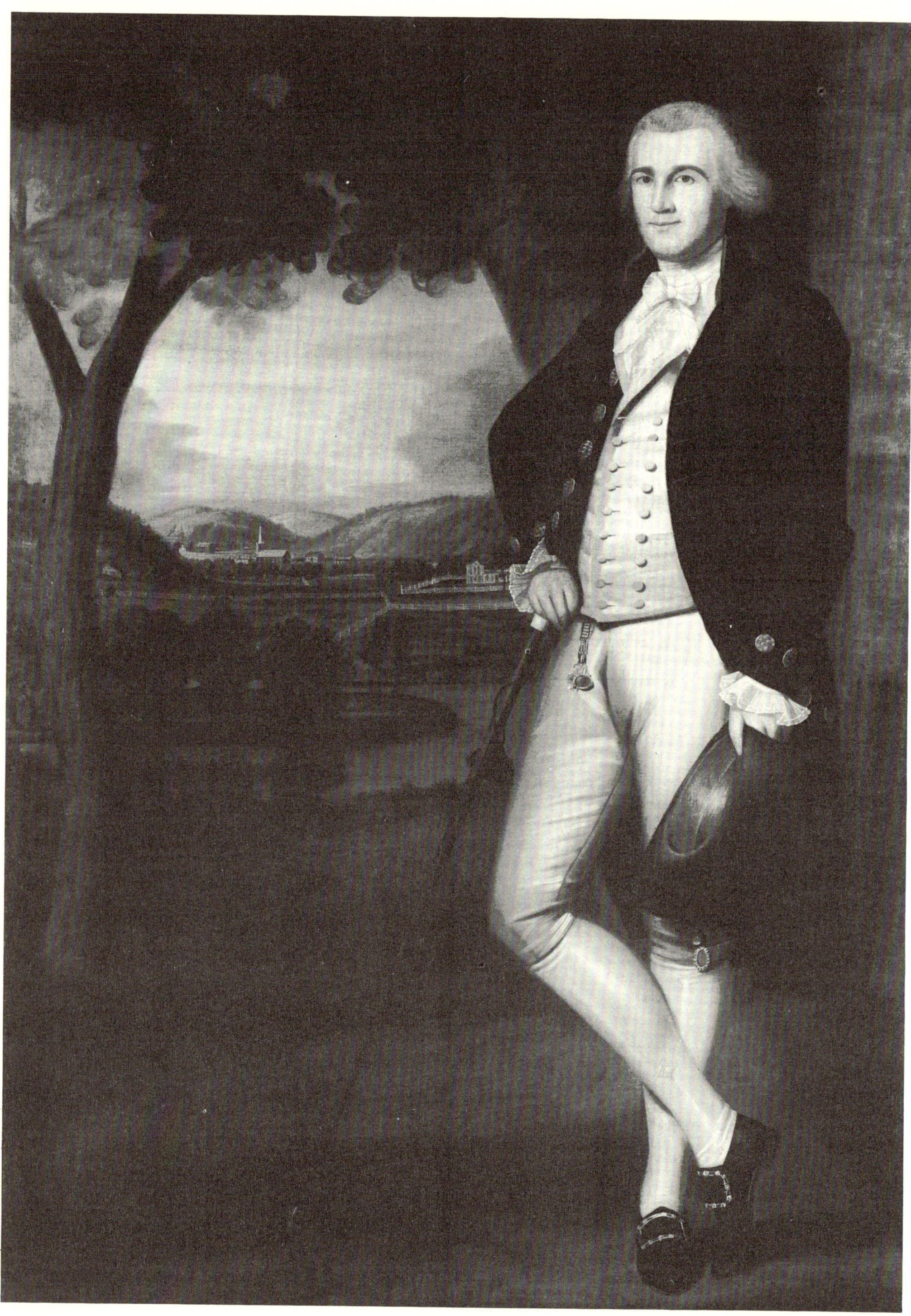

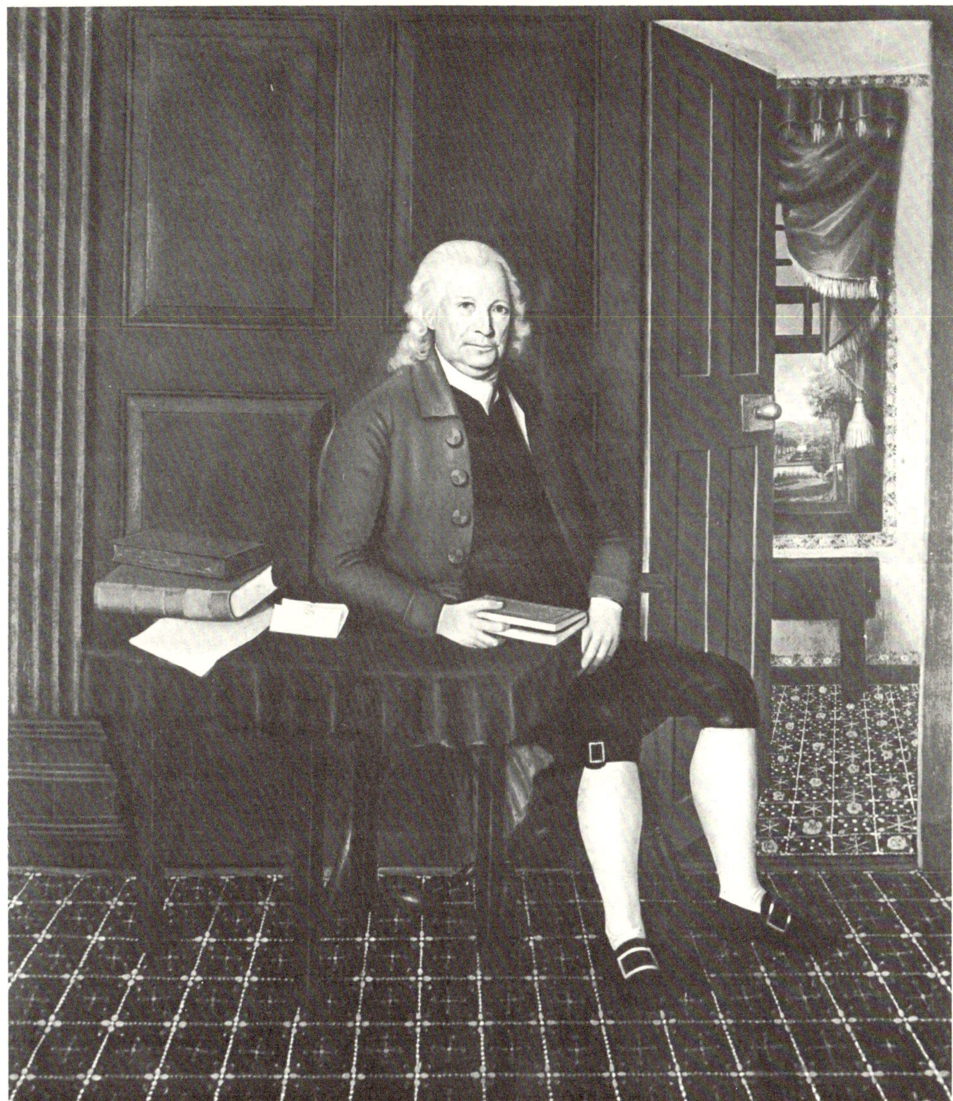

FIG. 13: Portrait of John Phillips by Joseph Steward.
Dartmouth College Collection.

FIG. 12 (opposite) : Portrait of Major Daniel Boardman
by Ralph Earl. *National Gallery of Art,*
Washington, D.C. Gift of Mrs. Murray Crane.

In addition to their role as source material for early overmantel painting, these fashionable early American portraits provide a helpful chronological reference for purposes of dating. Viewed from the perspective of academic portraiture, the overmantels in the Murdock-Pierce house can be attributed to the period around 1800. This conclusion finds additional support in the fact that Earl (1751–1801) and Steward (1752–1822), though mainly active in Connecticut, were both well-known figures in the upper Connecticut River Valley, where they were also known to have worked.[29] Indeed, it is even conjectured that Earl painted overmantels during his active career.[30] Finally, the Steward portrait of John Phillips was acquired by Dartmouth College in 1793 and would have been on display in New Hampshire directly across the river from the Murdock-Pierce house in Norwich.

5 · The Governor Galusha House

About the beginning of the nineteenth century the fashion for painting on wooden overmantel panels began to decline and was replaced by more indigenous (and expedient) forms of wall decoration. As witnessed by the mural in the previously discussed Murdock-Pierce house in Norwich, artists, in order to imitate overmantels, began painting directly on the dry plaster covering

[29] Earl did a landscape view of Bennington, Vermont, about 1776–78 (reproduced in Cummings, fig. 7). Steward was a graduate of Dartmouth College with the class of 1780.

[30] Nina F. Little, *American Decorative Wall Painting, 1700–1850* (New York, 1952), feels that "it is fair to suppose that Ralph Earl painted overmantels."

the chimney breast. At the same time this enabled them to dispense with the wooden panels.

Probably the earliest example in Vermont of the technique of painting on plaster in "distemper" (i.e., tempera) occurs in the Governor Galusha house at Center Shaftsbury in the southwest corner of the state (fig. 14).[31] The house was completed in 1809, the year that Jonas Galusha first became governor of Vermont, and its design is attributed to Lavius Fillmore, a Connecticut builder who came to Vermont in 1796.[32] A local tradition holds that the house served as an inn during the governor's lifetime.

In 1813 Galusha was defeated for the office of governor by the earlier mentioned Martin Chittenden of Jericho by a vote of the House of Representatives, history thus conspiring for our purposes to connect two of the important patrons of early Vermont wall painting.

The Galusha house overmantel is located in the southeast bedroom (fig. 14) and is the work of a highly skilled artist whose bold floral designs fill the entire surface of the chimney breast and extend as well to the adjoining walls of the room. The elegant floral pattern is executed free hand in dark outline against a dull green background. Characteristic features of the painter's style are a carefully controlled brushstroke and a keen sense of overall decorative harmony. These deft floral arabesques are, to be sure, more typical of the work of wall stencilers or embroidery designers than freehand mural decorators. As such, the work is more closely

[31] Congdon, p. 157 and fig. 123.

[32] This information was provided by Mr. T. D. Seymour Bassett, Curator of the Wilbur Collection of the Bailey Library at the University of Vermont in Burlington.

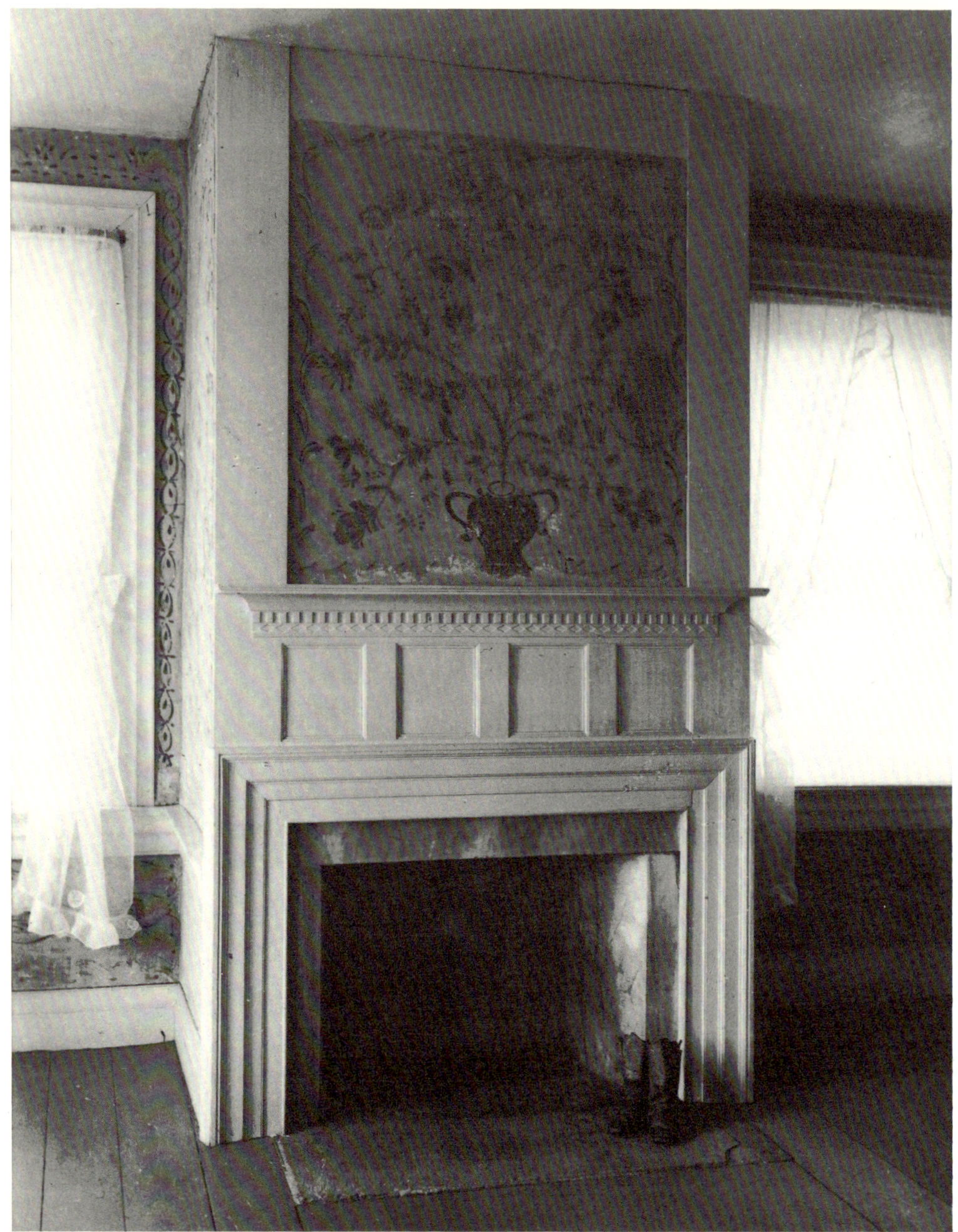

FIG. 14: Overmantel on plaster in the Governor Galusha House, Center Shaftsbury, Vermont. *Photograph courtesy of the Herbert W. Congdon Collection, Bailey Library, University of Vermont.*

allied to these decorative arts (where abundant examples of the vase and flower motif occur) than to scenic wall painting.[33]

According to legend, the painting was done by a wandering foreigner, either French or Italian, who ran up a sizable liquor bill at the governor's inn and did the decoration in partial liquidation of the debt.[34] Writing in the 1940s, one critic embellished these bare facts with the observation: "The erratic drawing of the patterns suggests a bountiful supply of the Governor's liquid assets as a source of both the debts and the inspiration of the artist."[35] Visions of *La Bohème* aside, the artist's finely controlled line, resulting in a true elegance of graphic design, is not easily reconciled with such facile judgments.

The seemingly indefatigable researches of Nina Fletcher Little have uncovered decorated walls by the same artist in several homes in Massachusetts and Connecticut.[36] At Northfield Farms, Massachusetts, however, the painter was, according to tradition, "a Frenchman who had deserted from the armies in the north at the close of the Revolution and had followed the Connecticut River to the vicinity of Deerfield."[37] Despite his reputed vices (drunkenness compounded by desertion), this widely travelled decorator was mainly active in the first decades of the nineteenth century and in point of time is more closely connected with the War of 1812 than the Revolution.

[33] Cf. Janet Waring, *Early American Stencils* (New York, 1937), fig. 31, for a stencilled chimneypiece with vases and flowers. See also Little, p. 95 and figs. 77–84, for similar decorations on fireboards.
[34] Congdon, p. 160.
[35] *Ibid.*
[36] Little, p. 94.
[37] *Ibid.*

Not least among the many treasures of American folk art in the National Gallery of Art, is a mural (fig. 15) salvaged from a recently dismanteled home in the vicinity of Ely, Vermont. It was presented by Edgar William and Bernice Chrysler Garbisch to the National Gallery in 1953, along with many other masterpieces of American primitive painting. A presumed date for the work is about 1825, and the high quality of painting ranks it among the finest surviving examples of early Vermont mural decoration. Enframed in what is considered the original wooden molding, the painting (26″ x 20¾″) was executed in tempera on plaster and probably served in its former location as an overmantel decoration.

The scene represented is a fairly typical combination of rural landscape with marine elements as seen, for example, in the Murdock-Pierce house in Norwich (fig. 7). In contrast to the earlier wooden overmantel, however, with its random assemblage of trees, houses, boats, and water, the painter of the Ely mural has employed the various elements of pictorial design to create a wonderfully balanced and integrated composition. In addition, the artist has eschewed the reliance of earlier overmantel painters on English prints or the schemes of fashionable American portraitists. Without renouncing the conventional iconography of sea and shore, the Ely painter has created a new and highly sophisticated style, perfectly adjusted to the function of mural decoration.

Though technically classified a primitive or folk artist, this early Vermont muralist displays none of the pictorial awkwardness

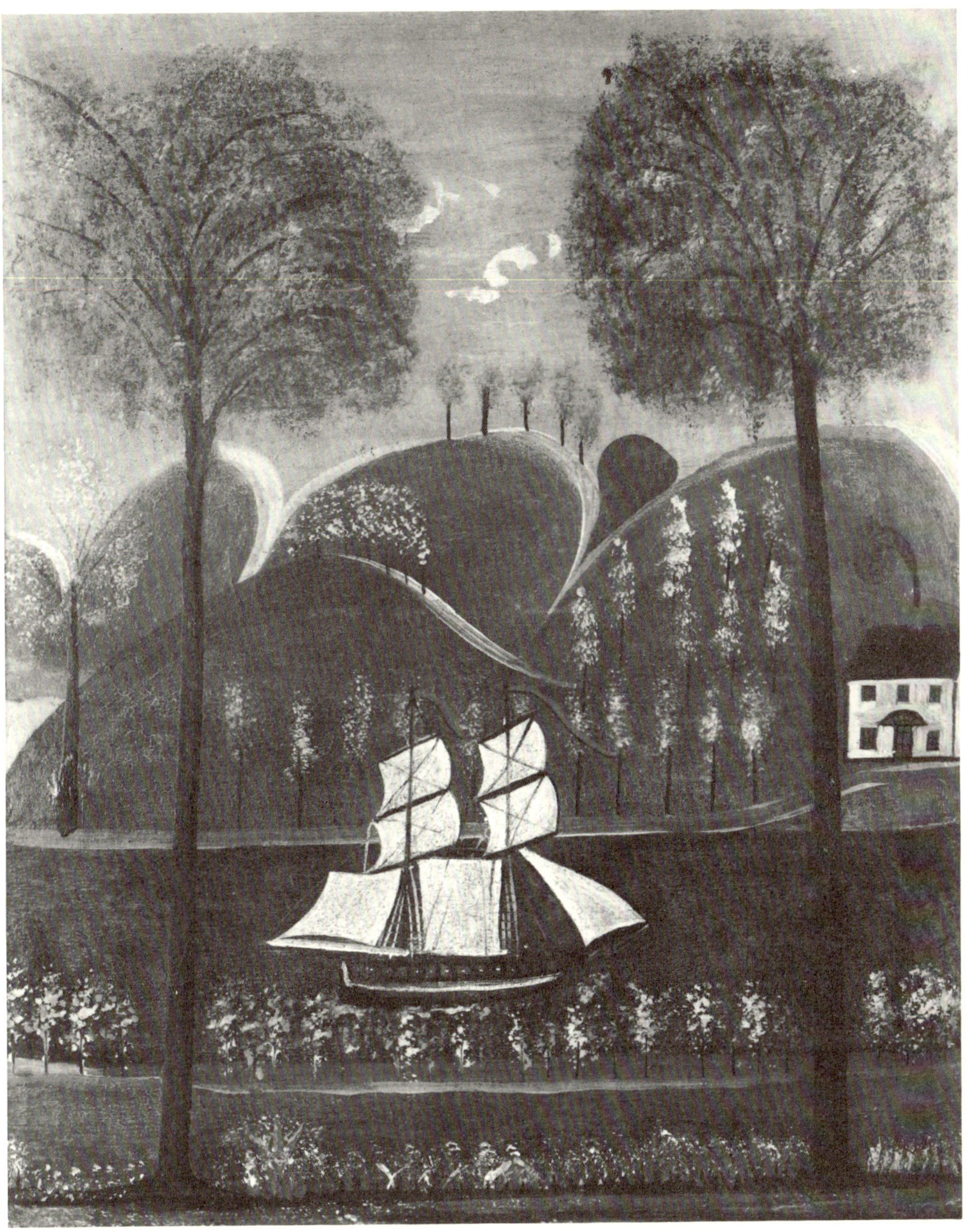

FIG. 15: "Under Full Sail." Overmantel on plaster from a house near Ely, Vermont. *National Gallery of Art, Washington, D.C. Gift of Edgar William and Bernice Chrysler Garbisch.*

or crudeness often associated with that style. His engaging design is, to be sure, both simple and uncomplicated, but the sureness of execution and the overall control of the composition reveal the touch of an instinctive master decorator. His colors are the inherited naturalistic greens, blues, and yellows, but unlike their use in pictorial antecedents, his chromatic scheme is employed to create surface patterns rather than integrated harmonies of atmospheric perspective. In similar fashion the painter uses a vertical perspective in order to emphasize surface and planar, rather than spatial, values. Consequently the abstract decorative appeal of the work takes precedence over illusionistic or naturalistic goals and frees the artist to distort forms and objects in the interests of decorative harmony.

Compositional balance is achieved by the strong verticals of the foreground elms employed to stabilize the dynamic horizontal movement of the mountains and river. Unusually bold and active brushstrokes are used to give directional flow to the course of the ship. A primitive "slip," however, can be seen at the right where a curl of smoke from the chimney of the house is activated by a wind blowing counter to that which propels the ship.

The basis for the Ely painter's style can no longer be sought in the official academic style of painting derived from European traditions. More likely its source is to be found closer to home in native American craft techniques. Committed to the decoration of surfaces rather than the creation of spatial illusions, the style of the Ely painter is more truly indigenous to early America than that of any of the works previously considered.

Above all, the style of the Ely overmantel is admirably suited to the function of architectural decoration. Rigidly stabilized by its design, the mural (could it be reintegrated into its original domestic setting) would enhance rather than deny the structure of the wall and thereby promote the unity of architecture and ornament. Unfortunately, no other works by this extraordinary artist have been discovered in Vermont or elsewhere in New England. His special awareness of the role of mural decoration, as well as the ornamental quality of his work, ranks him among the foremost early practitioners of the art. Finally, his work provides a strong anticipation of the style of Rufus Porter and thus constitutes an important link between painting on overmantels and the art of full-scale mural decoration.

CHAPTER III

Houses with Scenic Murals

I⊤ IS NOT POSSIBLE to state with certainty when the practice of large-scale scenic mural decoration came into use in New England. Frescoed walls have been found in the hallway of a fine home in Portsmouth, New Hampshire, which can be dated to the middle of the eighteenth century, but these appear to be an isolated instance of the art of mural painting in the colonies.[1] The Neapolitan painter Michele Felice Cornè, who came to this country in 1799, also decorated a number of homes in Massachusetts and Rhode Island with both overmantels and panoramic murals. His style, however, is derived uniquely from European sources and properly deserves little consideration as part of the native tradition of American folk art.[2]

[1] See Edward B. Allen, *Early American Wall Paintings, 1710–1850* (New Haven, 1926), pp. 21–25 and figs. 18–20; Nina F. Little, *American Decorative Wall Painting, 1700–1850* (New York, 1952), pp. 107–8 and figs. 128–29.

[2] For the career of Cornè see Allen, pp. 26–30, and Little, pp. 42–48. See also Katharine McCook Knox, "Note on Michele Felice Cornè," *Antiques,* LVII (1950), pp. 450–51.

Against this background, it appears that the art of mural painting in America developed autochthonously from the practice of
painting overmantels on plaster rather than from importation
from Europe. Beginning about 1800, another important factor in
the emergence of this new art form was the large-scale importing
of scenic wallpapers from France and England and the necessity
to create in America a cheap substitute for these expensive items.[3]
In this connection, such Yankee wall painters as Rufus Porter
were quick to advertise that the chief advantage of mural decoration over wallpaper is that the latter "is apt to get torn off, and
often affords behind it a resting place for various kinds of insects."[4]
In addition this practical-minded artist could point out that "the
four walls of a parlor can be completely painted in watercolors
[i.e., tempera] in less than five hours and at a total cost of ten
dollars."[5]

From these claims, however, it would be inaccurate to conclude
that early New England murals are simple imitations of imported
wallpapers. The native journeymen painters quickly developed
artistic means appropriate to their craft that bear scant relationship to the forms of decoration occurring on continental wallpapers.

Most scenic wall paintings in New England homes were painted
in the second quarter of the nineteenth century and are associated
with the figure of Rufus Porter and his school. Vermont, however,
is unusual in possessing several early examples of large-scale mural
decoration that precede the better-known Porter murals by one or

[3] See Little, pp. 99–101.
[4] Jean Lipman, *Rufus Porter, Yankee Pioneer* (New York, 1968), pp. 94–95.
[5] *Ibid.*, p. 95.

more decades. In addition, these works reveal that the art of mural painting was more widely practiced outside of the Porter milieu than is generally assumed.

In contrast to the painted overmantel, the full-length mural covers the entire surface of the wall and is no longer strictly ancillary to the architecture of the room and its permanent decorative scheme. Whereas chimneypieces provide a window view of an enclosed section of an imaginary painted world, murals have the property of dissolving the wall and substituting a total illusion—a second or pictorial reality as it were—for the reality of the room. Thus the space of the room can be amplified or restricted at the will of the artist, and the viewer can be made to merge both physically and aesthetically with the new painted environment.

1 · The Captain Dan Mather House

The exact date of the house that Major Timothy Mather built for his son Daniel in Marlboro is not known.[6] Timothy had come to Marlboro from Suffield, Connecticut, in 1774 at the age of sixteen and subsequently was to accumulate considerable wealth from a great variety of industries on the property.[7] It is most likely, however, that the house for his son Daniel was not completed until around 1810.

One of the local rumors has it that the painter who decorated

[6] Howard W. Congdon, *Old Vermont Houses* (New York, 1946), pp. 12–13 and fig. 10.

[7] See Ephraim H. Newton, *The History of the Town of Marlborough, Windham County, Vermont* (Montpelier, Vt., 1930), p. 209 for the history of the Mather family.

several of the rooms of the house with both murals and stencils was a deserter from the British Army in the War of 1812 and that he did the work in exchange for room and board.[8] Another source claims that the artist was actually a sailor who employed copious amounts of rum to enhance his impoverished artistic vision. According to this ingenious explanation, those parts of a room "done in the morning when the hand was steady show perspective and firm line, but by the end of the day when both head and hand had become uncertain, roofs began to take on new and strange angles."[9] Still another authority conjures up the ghost of Michelangelo by reporting that the work was done in secret with "no one being allowed to see the painter while at work."[10]

Of the original scheme, only the ground floor parlor retains its murals, the others having been papered over in recent years. The subject represented is the familiar New England countryside containing the customary trees, fields, and farmhouses (figs. 16 and 17) seen in many of the previously discussed overmantels. In the Mather house, however, the artist has enlarged the conception of the theme so that this conventional rural iconography now covers the entire surface of the four walls of the room from floor to ceiling. In consequence, the spectator is no longer confronted with the typical window view onto a landscape offered by an overmantel but has the simultaneous impression of being surrounded by nature and immersed within it. Large trees with slender trunks and prominent drooping branches press in on the room from all

---

[8] Allen, p. 65 and figs. 69–72. Allen reproduces some of the murals and stencils that have since been papered over.

[9] Janet Waring, *Early American Stencils* (New York, 1937), p. 78.

[10] Allen, p. 65.

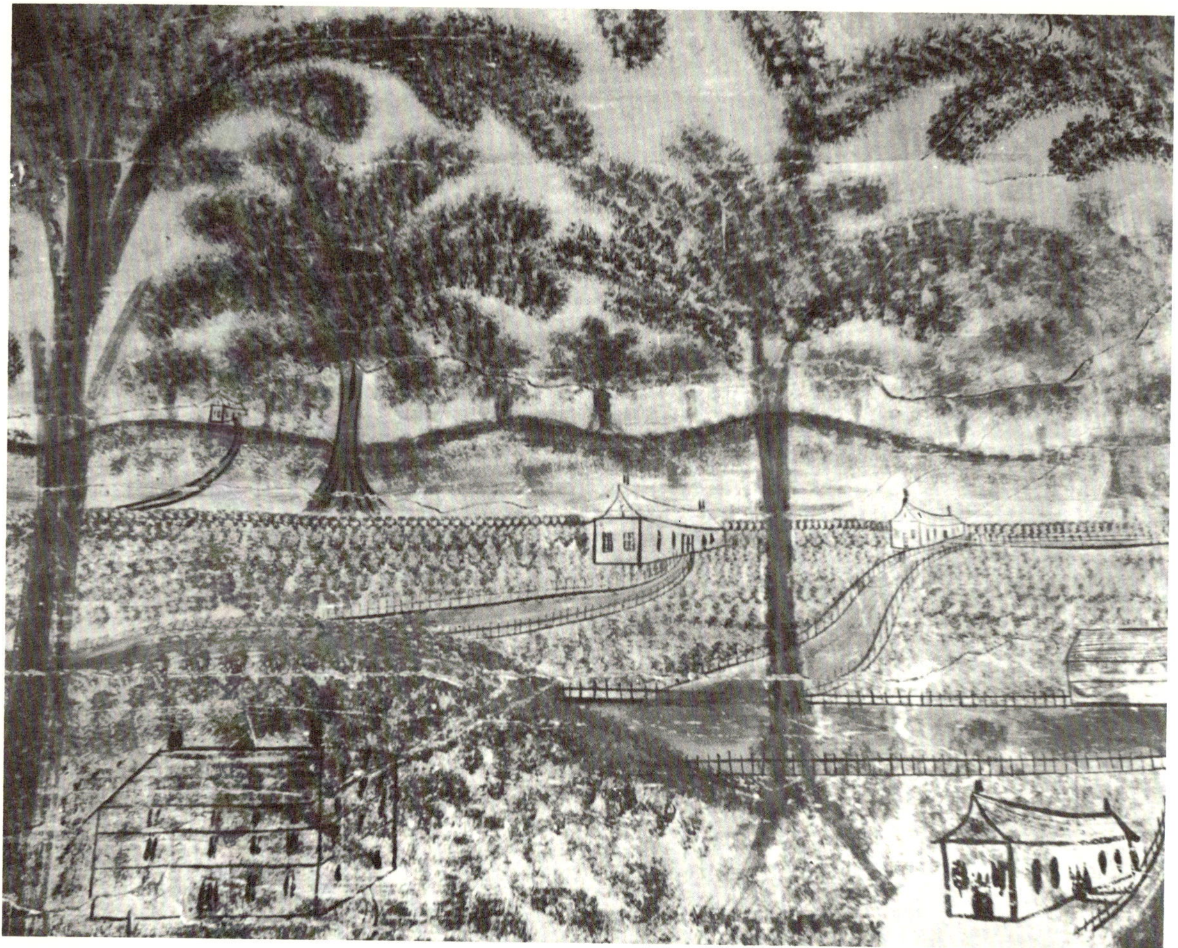

Fig. 16: Mural in the Captain Dan Mather House, Marlboro, Vermont. Compare the treatment of the trees and shrubs with the garden scene in figure 18. In both instances the muralist has substituted a barrier of foliage for the actual structure of the wall, thus creating a second wall of greenery which invites the spectator's attention and immerses him in an idealized world of nature.

sides in such a way that the parlor takes on the appearance of a clearing in a forest.

The impression is only momentary, however, for one soon realizes that these natural forms neither move forward nor recede into an illusionistic space. In the manner of the overmantel from Ely (fig. 15), objects have been piled one above the other to create a vertical perspective. The effect achieved is that of an opaque mass of foliage distributed in patterns over the surface of the wall. The impression is further enhanced by the artist's unusual technique of painting directly on the wall without any background save that of the white plaster.

Fig. 17. Mural in the Captain Dan Mather House, Marlboro, Vermont.

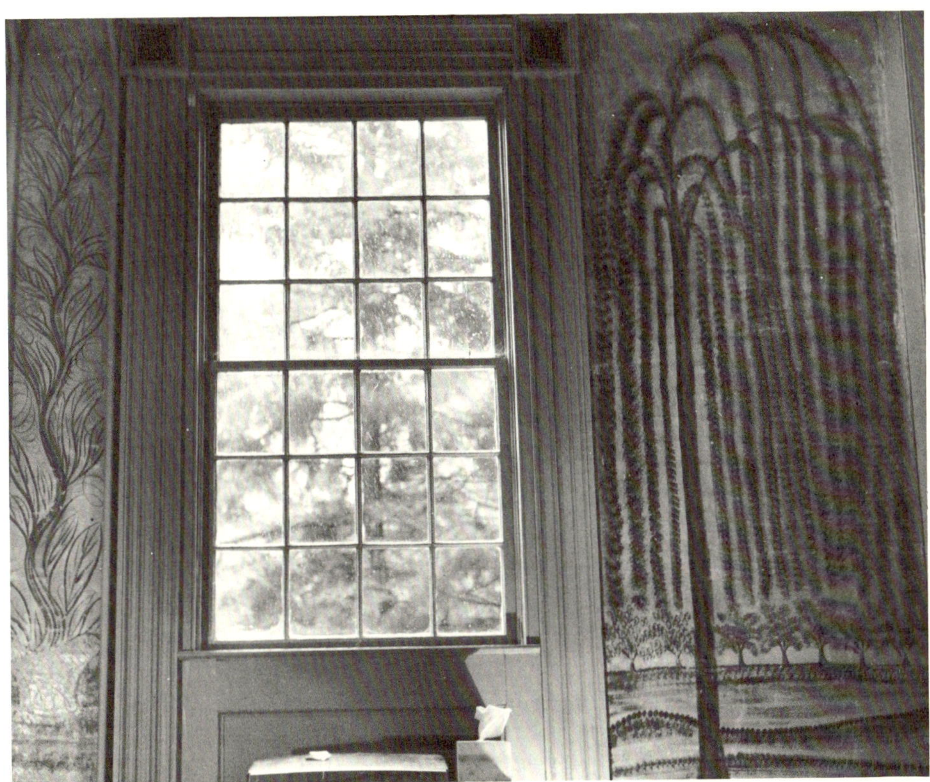

The lack of conventional perspective, which has engendered so much unfavorable critical comment with accusations ranging from drunkenness to incompetence, thereby appears less a question of artistic skill or alcoholic disability than a deliberate desire to fill the blank wall with forms for decorative rather than mimetic purposes. Thus the painted landscape becomes both an extension of the visible world of nature and a kind of enchanted fairyland made for looking and contemplating. In this connection another instructive comparison with ancient Roman painting is found in the famous murals from the Villa of Livia at Primaporta (fig. 18) from about 20 B.C. where the entire wall is also given over to the representation of a kind of ideal garden fairyland.[11] In this famous mural, one encounters a similar lack of perspective and a concern with surfaces rather than spatial values. Rather than pushing back the space of the wall, the ancient muralist has substituted a visual barrier of foliage which creates the impression (also found in the Mather house) of a second wall of greenery inviting the spectator's sympathetic view and involvement.

In his book on early American wall painting, Edward B. Allen connected the murals in the Mather house with a number of related works from neighboring states which he called the Connecticut River Valley group.[12] Paintings, as well as stencil work, from houses in Connecticut and Massachusetts were thought to be stylistically related and were attributed to an artist with the rather lurid appellation of "the Bernardston spy," because of his activity in that town on the Vermont-Massachusetts border.[13] According to

[11] On the Villa Livia and its mural decorations see Mabel M. Gabriel, *Livia's Garden Room at Prima Porta* (New York, 1955).

[12] Allen, p. 47.

[13] *Ibid.*, p. 63.

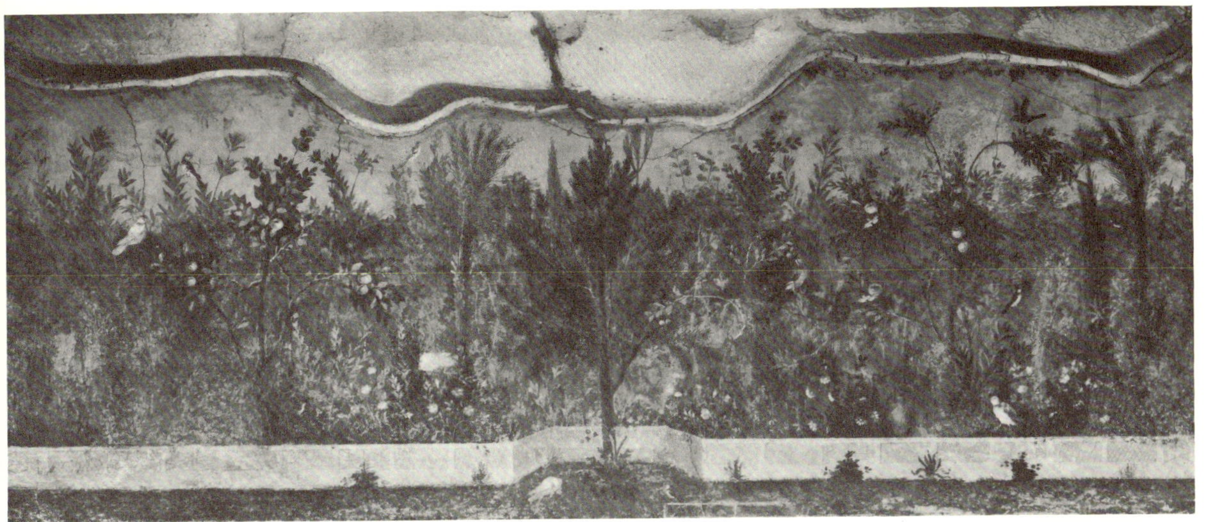

the legend, which has several variants, the artist came from "parts unknown" but was later apprehended by some men from Albany where he was taken and hanged as a spy.[14]

In her more recent publication, Nina Fletcher Little was able to unravel many of the details of the problem and to connect many of these murals with the figure of Jared Jessup, a resident of Guilford, Connecticut, who signed and dated at least one work in a home in Northford.[15] Though there is no evidence that Jessup was a British spy, it is certain that he travelled northward along the Connecticut River Valley between 1809 and 1813.

The murals in the Mather house, however, can no longer be convincingly attributed to the Jessup group. The discovery of wall

[14] Little, p. 93.
[15] *Ibid.*, pp. 87–93.

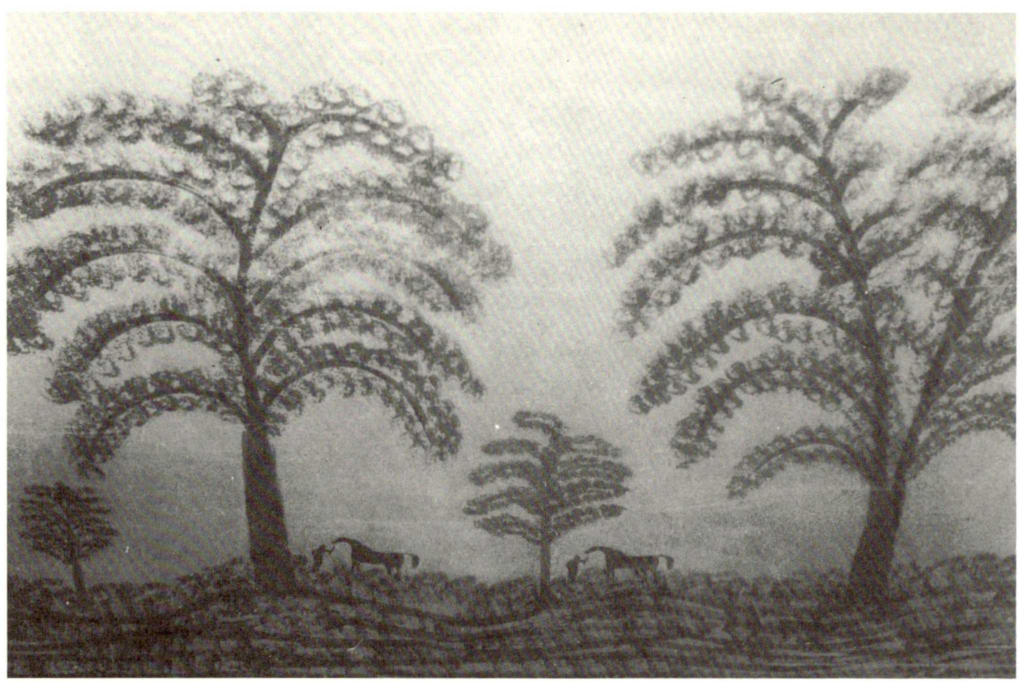

FIG. 19: Mural in the Burgess House, Sebec, Maine.
Photograph courtesy of Nina Fletcher Little.

paintings in a house in Sebec, Maine (fig. 19) reveals that the number of artists involved and the range of their activities were larger than previously supposed. Erroneously attributed at one time to Rufus Porter, the Sebec murals are moreover clearly by the same hand as those in the Mather house in Marlboro.[16] In all likelihood, these murals antedate Porter's earliest works by about a decade and, together with the Jessup group, constitute a sizable *oeuvre* attributable to several itinerant muralists previous to the better documented activity of Porter and his school.

[16] The Sebec murals were called to my attention by Nina Fletcher Little.

2 · *The Thompson-Schriftgiesser House*

The view that early American wall painting is mainly decorative in character, lacking any substantive narrative or historical content, can no longer be sustained. Evidence to the contrary is furnished by the recent discovery of a number of Vermont murals, of which one of the most problematic is found in a house in Londonderry (fig. 20). The house was built from native brick by a farmer named David Thompson and was probably completed around the year 1824. At least this is the date the present owner remembers having seen painted on one of the walls by the artist, presumably to signify the completion of his work.[17] In recent years this date, together with most of the paintings, has been papered over, though the name of the artist, Powers (he is called variously John or Thomas), has been kept alive in local legend.

Thomas Powers, as he is most usually called by residents of Londonderry with memories long enough to recall the tale, was a traveling artist who made his home in nearby Woodstock, Vermont. He is reputed, moreover, to have been the father of the famous neoclassical sculptor Hiram Powers (1805–1873).[18] He is also credited with a vivid and sanguine imagination for which, predictably, he found added sustenance in a bottle. From all reports the combination of art and alcohol in the blood was a formidable mixture; it was also the source of his downfall.

[17] Mr. Karl Schriftgiesser, the present owner of the home, assembled most of the facts concerning the artist Thomas Powers. For an account of the paintings see his article in the Boston *Evening Transcript,* October 16, 1926.

[18] For the genealogy of the Powers family see A. H. Powers, *The Powers Family* (Chicago, 1884). In this account there is no indication that Hiram's father Stephen (1736–1818), "a farmer who found difficulty in providing his family with the necessaries of life," possessed any artistic aptitude.

Despite his eventual ruin, the painter has left us a sobering composition in the overmantel on plaster (57″ x 36″) that is found in the downstairs parlor. Among the surviving early Vermont wall paintings, this work is the most thoroughly enigmatic with regard both to its author and its meaning. Depicted against a floral background are two figures arranged symmetrically on either side of a crouching lion. Above the beast is written in cursive script the strange epigram "The R. T." The figure at the left is an officer, clad in a blue uniform with gold borders and large epaulettes; he also wears a drooped cap with a flowered cockade. In one hand he holds an unidentifiable object, while with the other he grasps one end of a scroll or tablet that has been effaced by a more recent application of white plaster. Opposite the soldier is a dark-haired lady in a full flowing dress who holds the other end of the plaster rectangle. Stiffly posed, these unknown personages do not look at each other, though they are united by the formal composition and the object which they grasp in common.

From the individualized treatment of their faces, it is likely that the painter intended to depict actual personages. Because of a decorative synthesis of stylization and verisimilitude, attempts to identify the couple, either through costume or attributes, have met with no success. Suggestions have ranged from Napoleon and Josephine to the Prince of Orange and his wife, though no explanations are offered for the appearance of these august personages on the walls of a Vermont farmhouse. Other strained conjectures include Richard the Lion-Hearted and General Lafayette.[19]

[19] Richard R. Towne, "The Mysterious Murals," *Yankee Magazine,* March, 1968, p. 157.

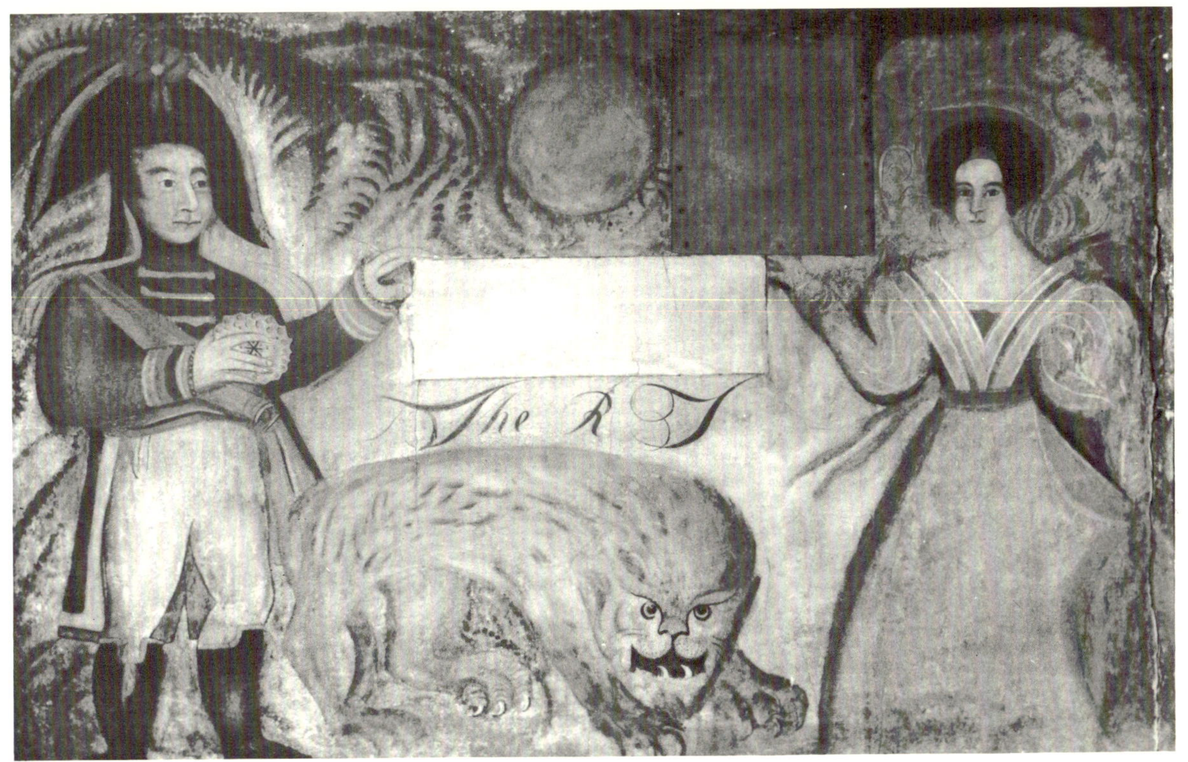

FIG. 20: Overmantel on plaster in the Thompson-Schriftgiesser House, Londonderry, Vermont.

Scarcely less intriguing, though no more credible, is the notion that the officer is the nefarious Count Rumford of Revolutionary infamy who, conveniently, was born Benjamin Thompson. Apart from the fact that this theory raises more problems than it solves, only a most foolhardy man would have risked this form of commemoration for the spy whose name was anathema to most early Americans.[20] A final pair of candidates are George and Martha

[20] See E. Larsen, *An American in Europe: The Life of Benjamin Thompson, Count Rumford* (New York, 1953).

Washington. Although the lion and the inscription hardly seem appropriate to them, they were represented on the wall of at least one home in Massachusetts.[21]

The real clue to the identity of the two persons doubtless lies behind the oblong of newer plaster which appears to have been placed there deliberately in order to disguise some evidence beneath it. A partial solution, however, to the meaning of the work, as well as a possible avenue of interpretation, is provided from a most unexpected quarter by Jan van Eyck's great wedding portrait of Giovanni Arnolfini and Jeanne Cenami in the National Gallery in London (fig. 21). In this masterpiece of fifteenth-century Flemish painting, one finds a similar symmetrical arrangement of the bridal pair about a central axis. The axis is composed of several objects, at least two of which (an animal and a florid inscription) are also present in the overmantel. Van Eyck's masterpiece thus appears to be, through some as yet unknown filiation, an iconographic ancestor of the Vermont mural. In short, the striking similarities in composition and subject found in the two works suggest that both descend from a common tradition for the representation of weddings and betrothals.

In further support of this contention, the dog, as used by Van Eyck, is a well-known symbol of marital faith and has for its counterpart in Christian art the lion, an emblem of masculine fortitude. The two symbols occur frequently in funerary sculpture where both husband and wife are represented.[22] Finally, the curious epigram on the overmantel, written in the elaborate script of a

[21] Little, p. 25.

[22] See the tomb of Jean the Fearless and the Duchess of Burgundy in the Musée de Ville at Dijon where the dog and lion serve as attributes, illustrated in Charles Rufus Morey, *Mediaeval Art* (New York, 1942), fig. 162.

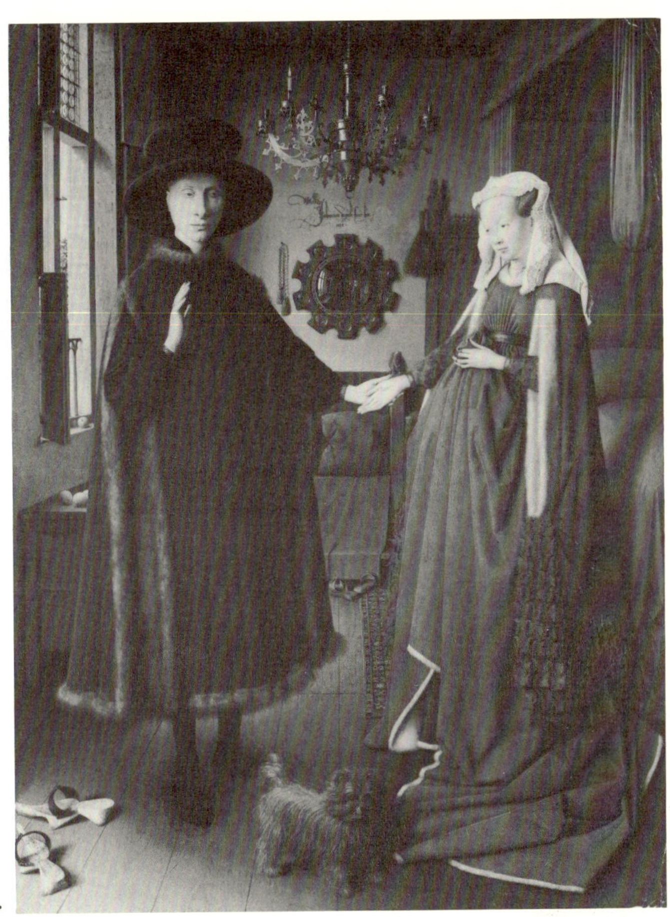

legal document, can be interpreted (in light of the use of script in the Flemish painting) as a form of testimony to the ceremony represented. From this perspective the Vermont overmantel is more comprehensible when viewed—like its more famous ancestor in London—as "both a double portrait and a marriage certificate."[23]

[23] Erwin Panofsky, *Early Netherlandish Painting* (Cambridge, Mass., 1953), p. 203.

Among the many distinctions between the two paintings, apart from obvious disparities in style and quality, are the gestures of the respective couples. Rather than joining hands to pledge their marriage vows, the Vermont pair probably held in common the marriage contract itself which appeared in the picture for all to see. It may be inferred that the later effacement of this area of the painting occurred as the result of a divorce or separation between the couple. As a result the legal function of the picture was nullified, and the portraits remained to puzzle future generations.

Investigation of the Thompson family genealogy has done nothing to reveal the identity of the officer and his presumed spouse or fiancée.[24] Neither David Thompson nor any of his many sons are known to have followed a military career, but the published accounts are far from thorough. Perhaps some future archivist will yet uncover the identity of the strange couple that stare out at us from this early Vermont wall.

In addition to the overmantel, the rest of the parlor was once filled with strange and unusual murals. Though the paintings are now papered over, a vivid description exists which renders their present state of eclipse all the more regrettable and prompts the hope that they will again see the light of day. According to this account the central figure on the wall opposite the fireplace was a large silver stallion:

> Never was a horse painted with more grace, no horse ever lived with so sleek a coat of shining gray hair. Nor does it seem possible that there has ever been a horse with such a noble and coal-black

24 See A. E. Cudworth, *The History with Genealogical Sketches of London-derry* (Montpelier, Vt., 1935), p. 188 for the Thompson family.

mane. He is slipping down a hillside and in his deep ebony eyes is
a haunted look of fear and despair that only a genius could impart.
There is reason for his fear and for his utter resignation to the in-
sane inevitable. For, on his arched back, there crouches a tiger that
is almost the incarnation of the Devil himself. His deep fangs sink
sharply into the silver skin of the horse. Blood, brilliant carmine
blood, spurts forth. The tiger is all steel and nerves, a nightmare
of a tiger from the very depths of the Heart of Darkness. No Congo
jungle ever held his fearful like. He has found his prey and the
taste of blood has sent him crazy. One glance and a shudder passes
through one.[25]

With allowances for journalistic hyperbole, one may nevertheless
infer that this was quite a startling mural. On another part of the
wall was a monkey hanging from a tropical tree engaged in drop-
ping coconuts into the open mouth of a shark. These nightmares,
it is claimed, were the product of a mixture of hard cider and New
England rum: "Caught in the grip of a mental frenzy which he
[the artist] could not conquer, he steadied his hand and painted
the hideous, demoniacal scenes. . . ."

Despite his unsavory reputation, the muralist appears to have
gained more than one commission on his tour of the Vermont
countryside. Writing in 1926, E. B. Allen described a house in
South Windham that "until recently covered with wallpaper was
frescoed with strange forest scenes in which serpents formed a very
prominent part, attracting immediate attention and holding one's
gaze fascinated with horror."

"It may have been the coiled monster which unintentionally
caused the story," Allen continues, "but the neighbors say the
room was painted by a wandering sailor who demanded a quart of

[25] Schriftgiesser.

rum a day besides his pay, and that the strange scenes were the result of a prolonged debauch."[26]

Still further traces of the bibulous artist appear in Windham proper where a lady reported in a recent issue of a popular magazine that she had a large mural papered over because she just "couldn't live with those scenes."[27] The mural contained a snake fighting with a saber-toothed tiger: "The snake is biting the tiger, and the tiger is clawing the snake. There is blood all over the place" the lady added, "it is pretty awful." These events, it is claimed, transpired against a tropical background containing, among other things, a volcano. The artist, one is gratified to report, was no tippler but a prisoner locked up in the house during the War of 1812.

Despite such fanciful description, these gory subjects are not unique to early Vermont wall painting, similar scenes having been found even at Pompeii.[28] Indeed, lions, tigers, and other tropical beasts of prey have exerted a strong influence upon the popular artistic imagination. Ranging from early American folk painting to more sophisticated works such as the Douanier Rousseau's magnificent painting of a lion slaying an antelope (fig. 22), such themes have always held a special place in the primitive repertoire.[29]

Formally trained artists were also responsive to these subjects. Despite the lack of stylistic affinity between the two works, a pos-

[26] Allen, p. 65.

[27] Towne, p. 157.

[28] See Maurizio Borda, *La pittura romana* (Milan, 1958), p. 287, for a Pompeian mural of a lion slaying a bull.

[29] See Little, fig. 75, for an early American fireboard with a ferocious predatory lion.

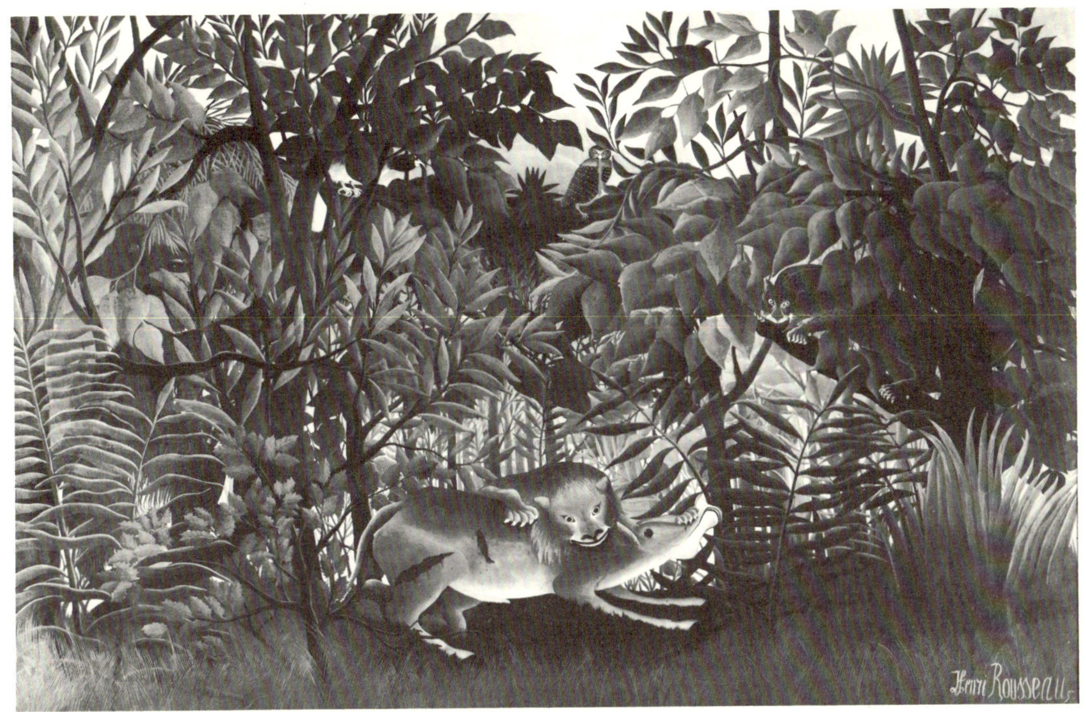

Fig. 22: "Lion Slaying an Antelope" by Henri Rousseau.
Private Collection, Zurich, Switzerland.

sible source for the mural in Londonderry of the tiger attacking a
silver stallion is the romantic masterpiece *Lion Attacking a Horse*
(fig. 23) by the English painter George Stubbs (1724–1806). Inspired by a trip to Morocco where Stubbs saw the actual enactment
of this scene, the painting was widely imitated for its novelty and
excitement. In this work, Stubbs reputedly created a "new type of
animal picture full of Romantic feeling for the grandeur and
violence of nature."[30] Stubbs's painting, together with the imita-

[30] Horst W. Janson, *History of Art* (New York, 1962), p. 467.

tions that it engendered, was well known in America, especially through prints and engravings.[31] In this connection Stubbs's work, rather than the often-cited bottle of rum, seems the more reliable source in attempting to account for the pictorial fantasies of Thomas Powers.

[31] For the career of Stubbs see Ellis Waterhouse, *Painting in Britain, 1530–1790* (Baltimore, 1953), pp. 205–10.

FIG. 23: "Lion Attacking a Horse" by George Stubbs. *Yale University Art Gallery, Gift of the Yale University Art Gallery Associates.*

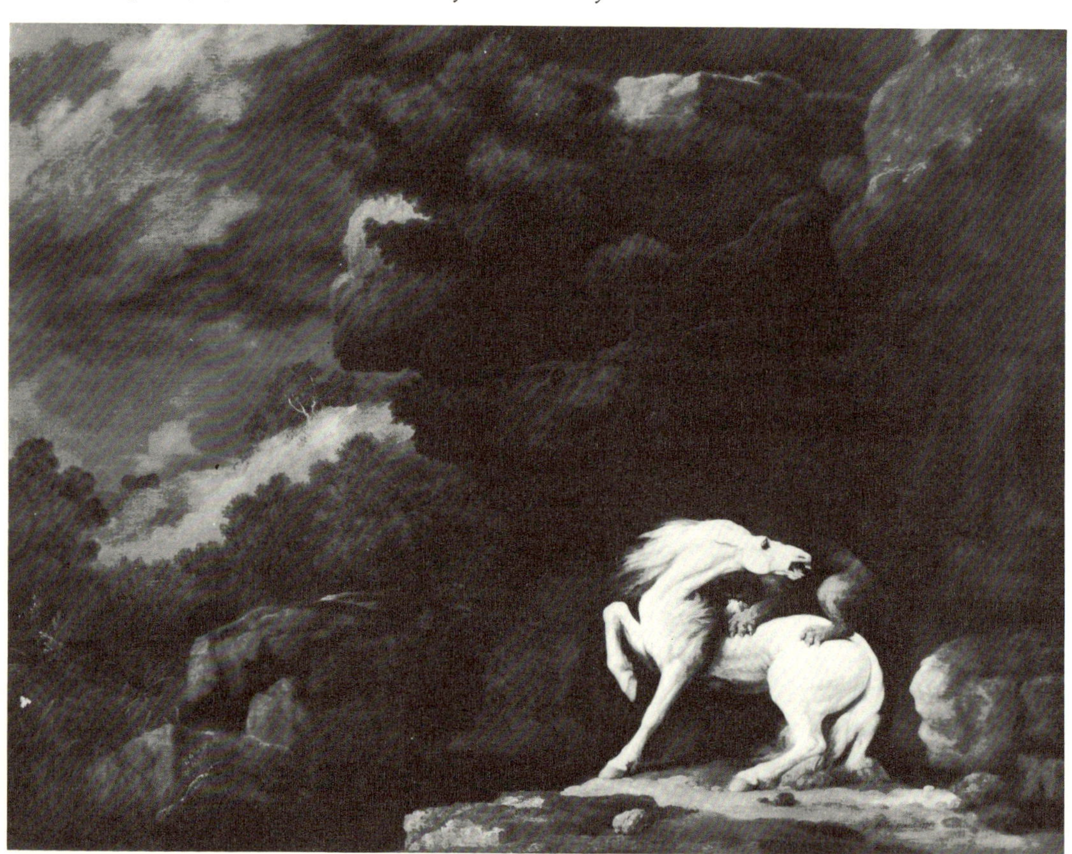

Any account of early American wall painting would be deficient without a consideration of the work of the nation's foremost early muralist, Rufus Porter (1792–1884).[32] Porter, it appears, worked in Vermont on at least one occasion, the result of which is visible on the walls of a home in the little town of East Topsham (figs. 24–27). The finest extant ensemble of Vermont decorative wall painting, the Topsham murals were only recently uncovered beneath several layers of wallpaper.[33] It is, however, a near certainty that Porter decorated other houses throughout the state, since over one hundred homes frescoed by the artist and his followers have been found in New Hampshire, Massachusetts, and Maine.

Rufus Porter has justifiably been called "the chief wall painter of his day and the most noteworthy mural painter in the history of American art."[34] He was, moreover, as his biographer Jean Lipman has aptly observed, "the most typically native and the most radically modern of the early landscape artists." Possessing a surer intuition for the art of mural decoration than any of his rivals, Porter brought to his craft a control and sensitivity to design and execution well beyond that of the average journeyman folk artist.

A kind of Yankee Leonardo da Vinci, Porter was also interested in science and technology and was the author of numerous inventions, ranging from a steamship to an aerial blimp.[35] Porter's career as a painter falls mainly into the two decades between 1825

[32] For Rufus Porter see Lipman.
[33] For the Topsham murals see Robert L. McGrath, "Rediscovery: Rufus Porter in Vermont," *Art in America*, LVI (1968), pp. 78–80.
[34] Lipman, p. 6.
[35] *Ibid.*, p. 27.

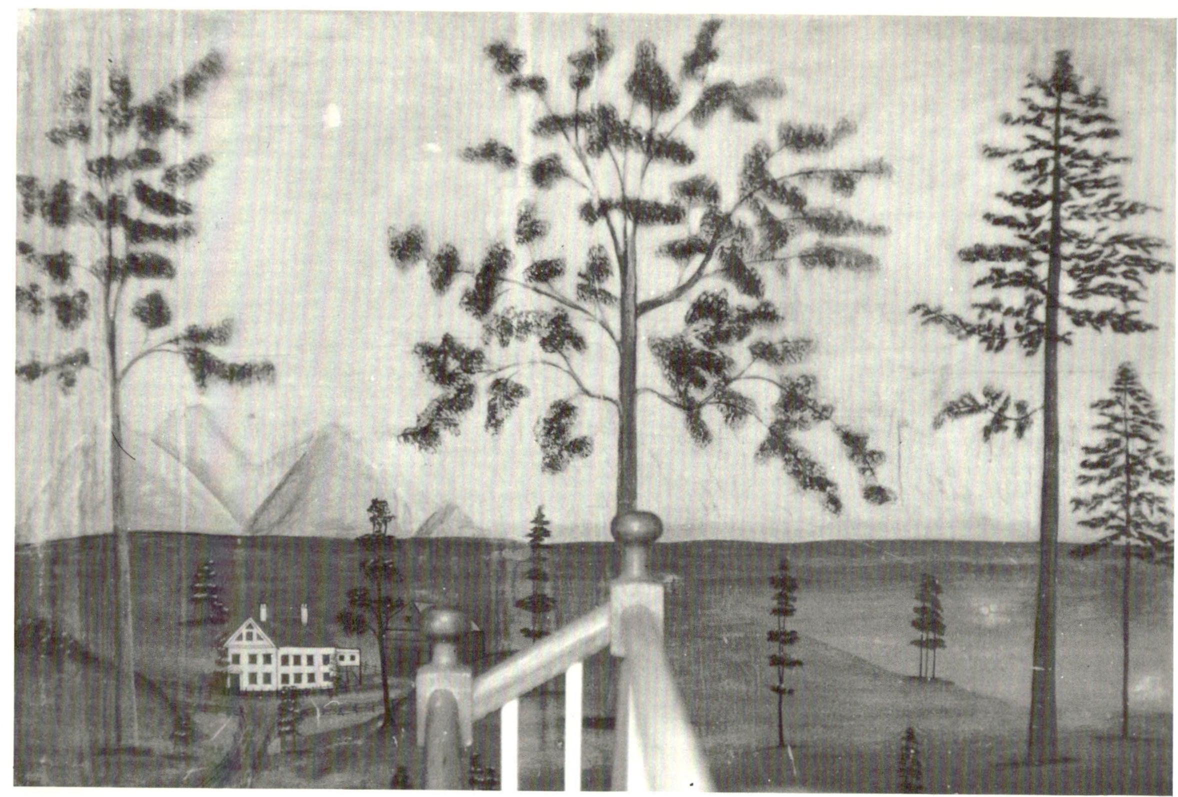

FIG. 24: Mural in the Chase House, East Topsham, Vermont.

and 1845. During these years he was active in the New England states, especially along the Connecticut River Valley.

The distinctiveness of Porter's style suggests that he was largely self-trained, though the previously discussed overmantel painting from Ely (fig. 15) does provide a strong foretaste of the high quality of his best work. Porter's murals, however, are more spatial and illusionistic than the Ely overmantel and the range of colors employed is generally richer and more varied. Indeed, the special

70

appeal of his work derives largely from a deliberate synthesis of the illusionistic properties of overmantel painting with the patterned-planar qualities of earlier frescoes. In all instances his work is admirably adjusted to the function of mural decoration.

The Topsham murals are not Porter's most ambitious decorations, but in their bright state of preservation, they reveal the artist at his most characteristic. Appearing in both the downstairs and upstairs hallways, the paintings cover the wall from floor to ceiling and are organized along the staircase to create the illusion of a descending mountain slope.[36] The end walls contain landscapes,

[36] See Lipman, figs. 77, 80, and 81, for some Massachusetts homes decorated with similar schemes.

FIG. 25: Detail of mural in the Chase House, East Topsham, Vermont.

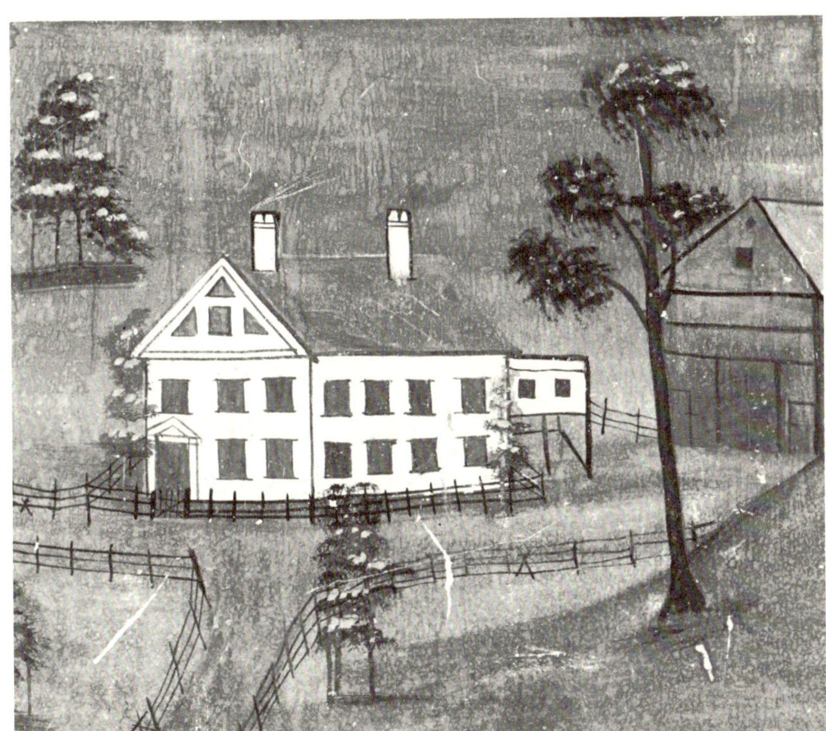

while the southernmost walls, both upper and lower, are given over to marine subjects. This thoughtful attitude toward the walls of the house in terms of composition and subject is typical of Porter's work, as are the simple emphatic designs and the bright primary colors used to create his delightful scenes of sea and shore.

In addition to his painting, Porter is noteworthy for a series of writings in the *Scientific American* (the journal that he founded and edited) on the practice of mural decoration. In these essays he stated that it was not necessary to imitate nature in order to create effective mural decorations.[37] This seemingly ultra avant-garde view for a provincial nineteenth-century painter has been noted by Jean Lipman who further commented on Porter's "desire to 'excel nature itself' in the interest, clarity, and brilliance of design and color." This, it is claimed, largely accounts for "the contemporary look of his deliberately stylized landscapes."[38] In addition to this testimony, Porter's independence from the demands for conventional realism is further evidenced by the works themselves which aspire less to visual integration and the harmonies of atmospheric color common to academically trained artists, than to the decorative probity derived from the native American craft tradition.

The contents of the Topsham murals, both landscapes and marine subjects, are drawn from Porter's repertory of standard formulas and may well have been made with the assistance of patterns or "theorems" for such items as ships and farm buildings.[39] Despite the general view that Porter was merely a decorator, he appears in

[37] *Ibid.*, p. 98.
[38] *Ibid.*
[39] See Lipman, p. 97, for Porter's discussion of the use of patterns.

72

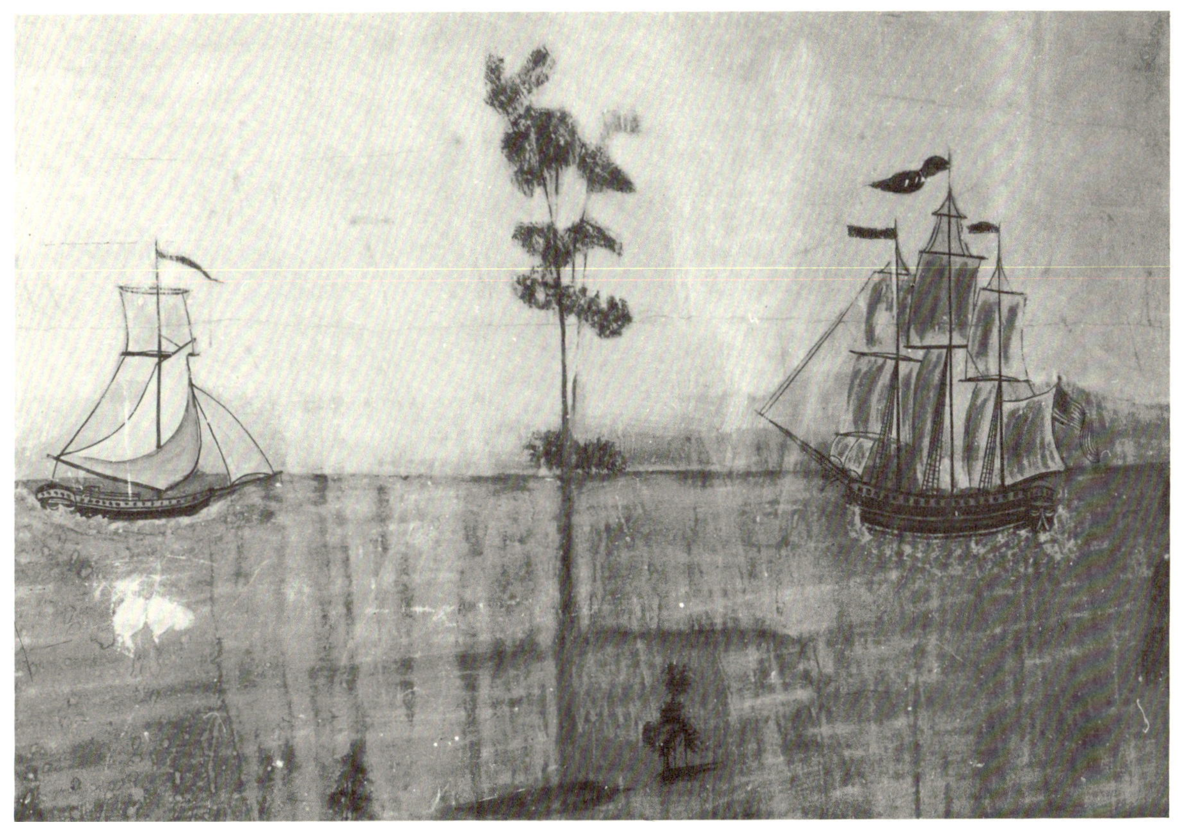

FIG. 26: "The Potomac." Detail of mural in the Chase House, East Topsham, Vermont.

the case of the Topsham murals to have brought along some specific narrative baggage for the large marine painting in the upstairs hall (fig. 26). Fortunately, a search for the facts that lay behind this seemingly conventional representation of two sailing vessels proved successful and provides an account of real interest and unusual topicality for the student of American history.

Against a golden sunset sky, a three-masted vessel advances

73

through a tranquil blue sea, her red pennants fluttering on winds opposed to those activating the national flag. Running before a full breeze, the logical source of which is blissfully ignored, a sloop is about to cross her bow. The larger ship, as the pennant from the main mast informs us, is the U.S. frigate *Potomac* while the commodore's pennant obligingly provides her captain's name, Downes. Nautical experts will recognize the *Potomac* as the first of the famous forty-four-gun frigates to the command of which a certain Captain John Downes (1784–1854) was appointed, as the records inform us, on May 9, 1831.[40] These are the basic facts but it is doubtless the famous globe-circling cruise of the *Potomac* between the years 1831 and 1834 that prompted the unusual inclusion of specific references in the painting. If the contemporary accounts are to be accepted, the cruise of the *Potomac* precipitated a major *cause célèbre* of the day, one that would have appealed to Porter, himself a former seaman.[41]

According to the accounts, both official and unofficial, Commodore John Downes was dispatched in May of 1831 by the secretary of the navy to seek redress from the natives of Quallah Batto, a trading village on the island of Sumatra, for a "murderous attack" of the previous February against the merchant vessel *Friendship* out of Salem. Almost exactly one year from the date (February 5, 1832) of this "wanton outrage," Downes entered the harbor flying the colors of a Danish merchant ship in order to disguise his

[40] See "A Sketch of the Life of John Downes, Esq., of the United States Navy," *American Monthly Magazine,* VIII (1836), p. 71.

[41] There are two major published accounts of these events: Francis Warriner, *Cruise of the United States Frigate "Potomac" Round the World* (Boston, 1835) and Jeremiah N. Reynolds, *Voyage of the United States Frigate "Potomac"* (New York, 1835).

true purpose and identity. The next morning, and at a cost of but two men, the commodore launched a ground attack upon the town, accompanied by a barrage from his thirty-two-pound cannon. The unannounced assault came as a complete surprise; some hundred Malays were killed or wounded and by noon the American flag was hoisted over Quallah Batto. Historians, incidentally, have established this event as the first American military engagement in the Far East, a harbinger of later and more tragic events.

When news of Downes's rather summary action against these natives reached the States in July of 1832, it created a considerable stir in liberal circles that resulted in a full congressional hearing.[42] But Downes was totally exonerated on the grounds that the offenders were "a race of a character so lawless and savage as not to come within the scope of regular diplomatic intercourse." President Jackson, characteristically, gave his full approval to the conduct of the affair, commending Downes for his incisive action. The latter, however, was placed on waiting orders and never again given command of a ship, ending his career in charge of the Brooklyn Navy Yard.

While Porter may have been serenely oblivious of these proceedings in painting his scene, it appears more likely that the rare inclusion of names for the mural was prompted by familiarity with the events. There is sound reason to believe that the Topsham murals are a visible reminder of sentiments, either Porter's or possibly those of his patron, that recall vividly the era of Jacksonian expansionism, military protectionism, and an aggressive policy in foreign economic affairs.

[42] See *American State Papers, Documents, Legislative and Executive of the Congress of the United States,* Vol. IV *Naval Affairs,* Washington, D.C., 1861, p. 150–53 for the proceedings against Downes.

With respect to the dating of the murals, it seems most likely that Porter painted them in 1832 or 1833 when interest in the *Potomac* affair was at its height, although two published accounts of the cruise appeared as late as 1835.[43]

The true value of Porter's art, however, resides not in the chance historical associations which they evoke, but in the high quality of those designs which so brilliantly enliven the walls on which they appear. Opening up the room to all sides, they permit the enclosed interior space to merge through the special magic of Porter's art with the exterior world. At the same time probably no American muralist was more keenly aware of the role of his decorations in relation to the architecture itself. As Jean Lipman has observed apropos of Porter's work, "The painted perspective amplifies the room and the color lightens it, and still the decoration emphasizes the structural lines of the wall."[44]

These qualities are especially visible in the Topsham murals where Porter employs a careful balance of verticals and horizontals in order to stabilize the compositions and at the same time to promote an equilibrium between the surface and spatial values within the work itself. It is, above all, the "fine functional relationship" of the decoration to the wall that enables Porter's murals to rival the finest achievements of ancient Roman painting.

[43] See note 41.
[44] Lipman, pp. 145–46.

FIG. 27 (opposite): Detail of mural in the Chase House, East Topsham, Vermont.

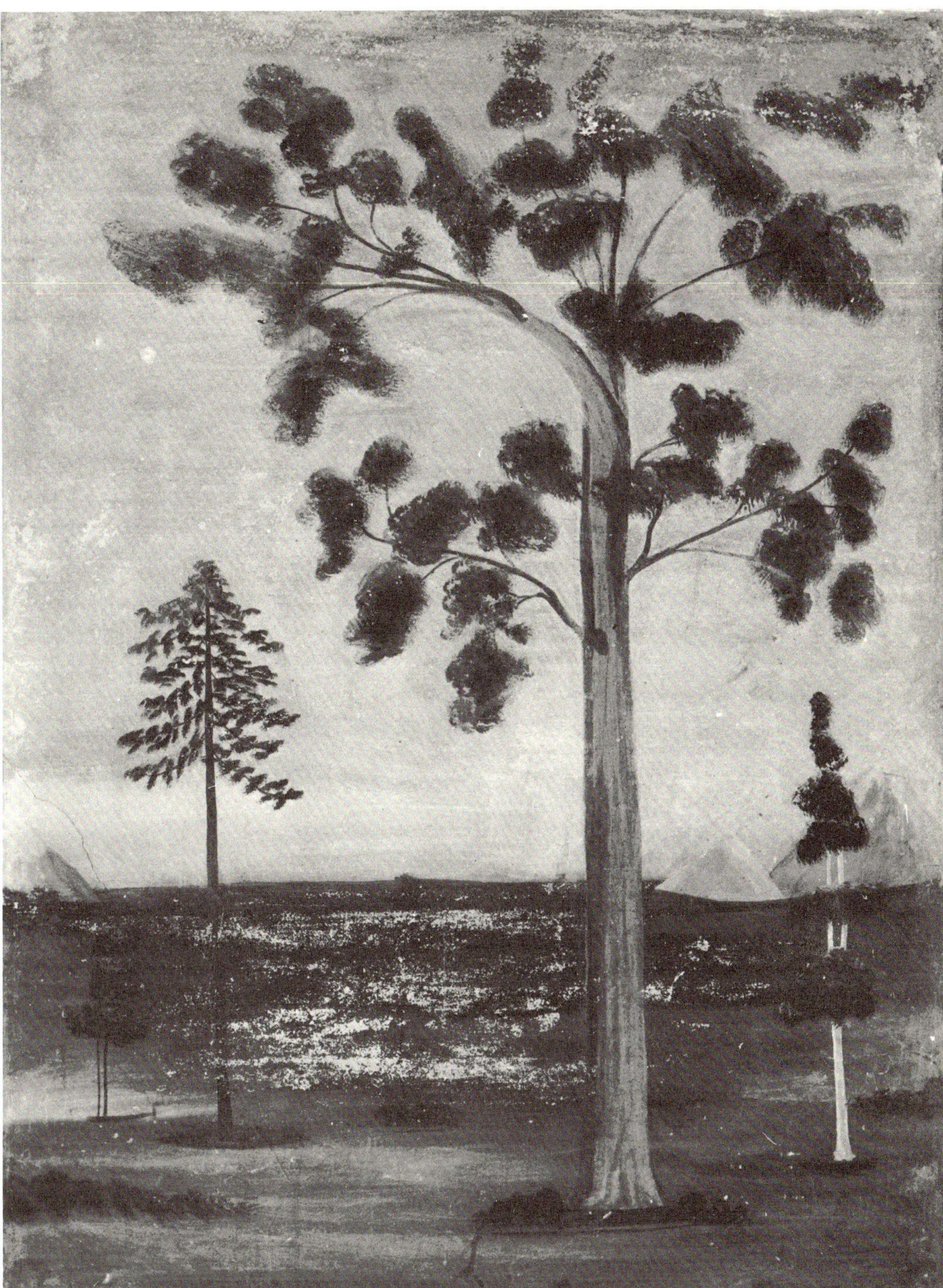

When, toward the middle of his life, Rufus Porter abandoned the career of an itinerant wall painter in order to devote his remaining energies to invention, he left behind a sizable group of pupils and assistants. The difficult task of sorting out the respective styles of these followers need detain us only briefly, for no murals by either Jonathan Poor or Orison Wood, Porter's chief imitators, have been found in Vermont.[45] An old house in Townshend, however, contains a series of curious wall paintings that bears a clear, albeit puzzling, relationship to Porter's *oeuvre* (fig. 28) .

Discovered a few years ago when some old paper was removed from the parlor walls, the murals display the characteristic stamp of Porter's affection for such exotic subjects as active volcanoes and tropical vegetation.[46] Other typical Porter school formulas include a squirrel in a tree and the motif of the trunk of a dead tree lying in the crotch of another.[47]

For these thematic reasons there can be no doubt that the Townshend muralist was familiar with Porter's work, although there is little possibility of confusing the style of his paintings with that of the master. Whereas Porter's murals, and those of his known followers, are deliberately stylized for purposes already described, the Townshend murals are governed by a desire to imitate nature closely; to create the illusion of appearances rather than to establish—in the manner of Porter—a decorative harmony

[45] *Ibid.,* p. 142, for a discussion of Porter's chief followers and assistants.

[46] See Lipman, fig. 91, for the typical tropical vegetation that is thought to be a souvenir of Porter's early visit to Hawaii.

[47] See Little, fig. 145, for the squirrel motif; Lipman, figs. 96 and 97 and pl. 21 for the dead tree.

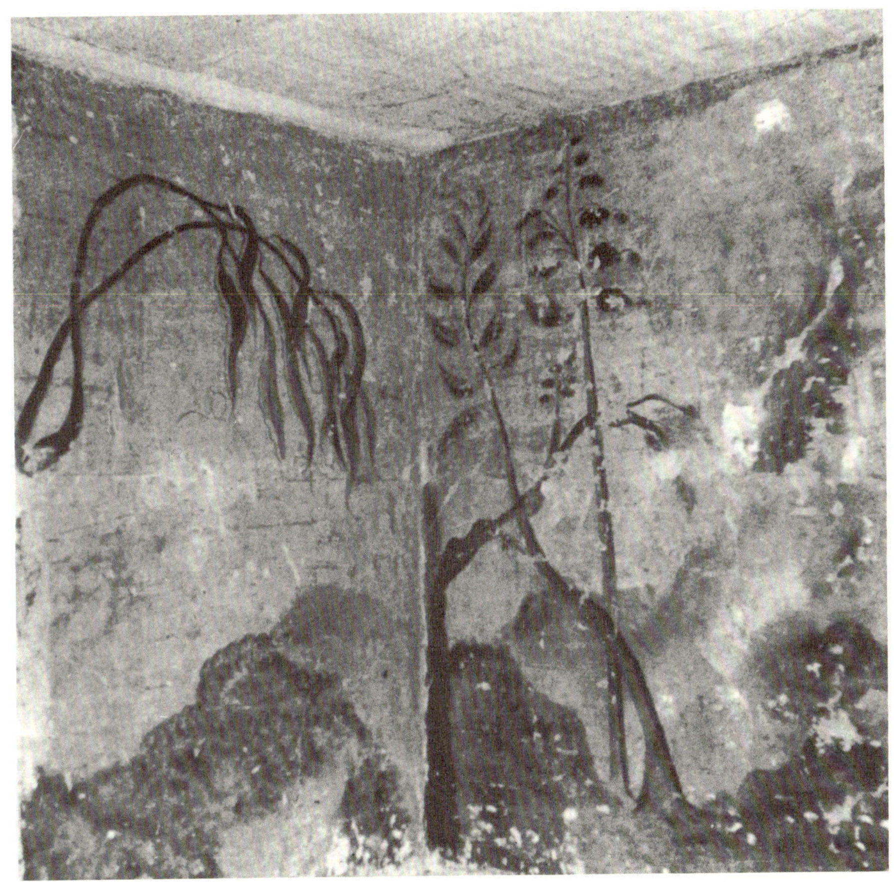

FIG. 28: Murals in the Lyman-Twitchel House, Townshend, Vermont.

parallel with nature. There are, in addition, a number of other independent (i.e., non-Porter school) features in the work at Townshend including a delicate grapevine painted between two of the windows and some very original scrollwork along the wainscoting.

In the matter of attribution, there are, predictably, no less than three local variants of the legend concerning the painter of these murals. They are ascribed, in no particular order of importance, to the familiar prisoner (War of 1812), the ubiquitous itinerant, and the habitual drunk.[48] With unprecedented specificity, however, the tippler was one Colonel Jonas Twitchel, a former owner of the house, who reputedly went on a painting spree brought on by an excess of spirits. Twitchel had bought the house in 1831, according to the records, and the paintings probably date some ten to fifteen years later. Happily, the Colonel was recently exonerated through the efforts of a local historian. Though not all judges are sober, nor all lords drunk, Colonel Twitchel, as president of the local bank, emerges from these findings as an unlikely candidate for muralist, "drunk or sober."[49]

To date no other paintings in the unusual style of the Townshend muralist have come to light either in Vermont or the other New England states. The artist was, almost certainly, a student or follower of Rufus Porter, although, as previously noted, the formal or stylistic source for his work certainly derives from elsewhere. In contrast to Porter's sharp and emphatically linear designs, the Townshend muralist employs soft rounded forms and blurred edges in order to evoke "painterly," atmospheric effects. Where Porter tended to Americanize such alien subjects as erupting volcanoes, the Townshend painter revels in the bizarre and exotic aspects of these subjects which he burdens heavily with romantic overtones.

[48] See Richard R. Towne, "The Mysterious Murals," *Yankee Magazine,* March, 1968, p. 88.
[49] *Ibid.,* p. 89.

In lieu of the early American mural style, the source for the paintings at Townshend is probably to be found in such imported wall papers as the fashionable set illustrating "Pizarro's Conquest of Peru," which was popular in this country throughout much of the early nineteenth century.[50] In such voguish items as the Pizarro paper or the equally famous "Bay of Naples" series, one encounters many of the same smoking volcanoes, tropical flora, and lush ambience that are featured so conspicuously in the Townshend murals.[51]

In a larger sense the departures from the Porter style observed in these paintings are of a profoundly fundamental nature. Where Porter strove to create a viable and formally autonomous substitute for the expensive imported wallpapers, the Townshend muralist seeks to imitate them outright. No longer invested with the formal and stylistic integrity of the best Porter murals, the Townshend paintings indicate a basic alteration in the character of the art form. In large measure the eventual decline of the indigenous Yankee craft of wall painting can be attributed to the transformations observed in these murals.

In short, the Townshend murals are indicative of a shift in popular taste away from the native aesthetic towards the bizarre and romantic. Revealing a new affection for the exotic, these paintings no longer aspire to the decorative clarity of Porter school murals. In place of the simple New England countryside favored by Porter and his followers, a kind of florid hothouse landscape

[50] See Kate Sanborn, *Old Time Wall Papers* (Greenwich, Conn., 1905), pl. XXXV.

[51] The imitation of foreign wallpapers was also practiced by the early muralist Cornè. See Little, p. 118, for a mural imitating the Bay of Naples.

that conjurs up visions of primordial rain forests and steaming tropical jungles is offered. As such the Townshend murals provide an ample foretaste of that vogue for things strange, "romantick," and foreign that by midcentury was to engulf many aspects of American popular culture.

CHAPTER IV

Mural Painting
in the Later Nineteenth Century

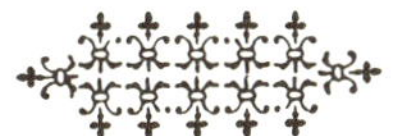

THE virtual disappearance of the art of the itinerant wall painter in the second half of the nineteenth century has been attributed to the invention of cheap marketable wallpaper.[1] Though the popularity of these machine-printed papers did, in fact, contribute much to the demise of the art form, a more decisive cause is probably the previously described transformation of popular taste which occurred about midcentury. Arising from such movements as the neoclassical, gothic, and romantic revivals, this phenomenon relied heavily on the style of past cultures and created a corresponding aversion to the native American aesthetic. The indigenous style of wall decoration, represented at its height by Rufus Porter, became no longer acceptable to a pretentious Victorian middle class which after 1850 looked increasingly to Europe for tutelage in cultural affairs.

[1] See Nina F. Little, *American Decorative Wall Painting, 1700–1850* (New York, 1952), p. 125. The first machine for printing wallpapers was imported into this country in 1844.

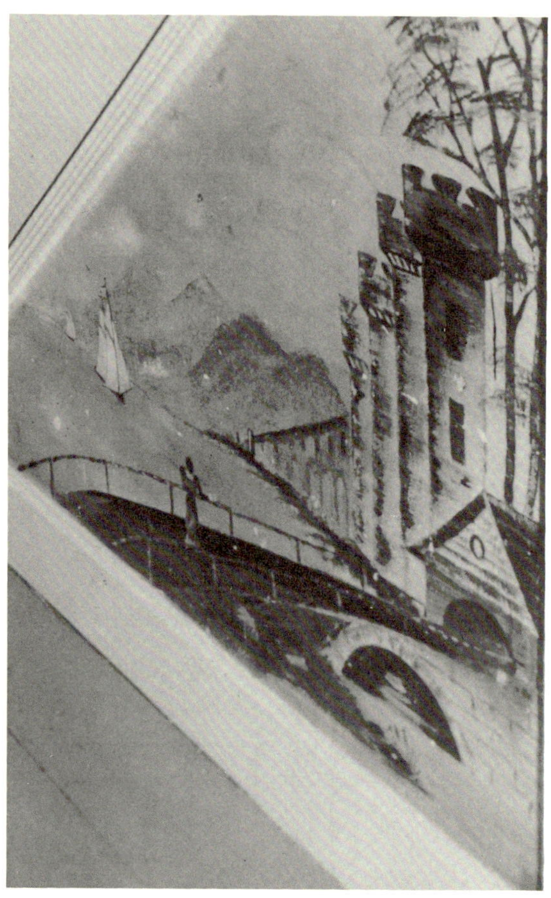

FIG. 29: Mural in the
Benjamin Wales House,
Weybridge, Vermont.

Despite the determined efforts of such landscape artists as
Church, Cole, and Bierstadt (and other painters of the Hudson
River school) to counter this movement, the history of American
art from midcentury on is in large part the imitation of foreign
styles. Myriad pretensions often blinded artist, critic, and con-
sumer alike to the virtues of the native style. In Vermont the story

is not much different from elsewhere in America, though social and economic conditions did conspire in some instances to immunize the state against some of the less desirable products of these revivals.

To date, only a few examples of later nineteenth-century mural decoration have come to light in Vermont, though in each case the extent of the decline of the art form is plainly revealed. The Benjamin Wales house in Weybridge, for example, was built in the 1860s and contains a curious mural (fig. 29) painted on the triangular field of plaster beneath the hall staircase. The present owners report that it was the work of an itinerant about the time of the Civil War who painted it for room and board.

The mural is a crude provincial interpretation of what appears to be a European scene, possibly the coast of the Mediterranean or the English Lake District. Castles with crenellated parapets, covered bridges, and languid ladies staring out to sea form the basis for this wistful and eclectic panorama. At best, the work brings to mind the painted idylls of the Neapolitan Cornè rather than the less emotive products of the native school of muralists.[2] Again, the source for the mural can probably be located in any number of romanticized scenic wallpapers imported from France where similar compositions occur.[3]

Another work of approximately the same date and containing similar thematic elements (castle, water, boats, and small figures) comes from the previously discussed Governor Chittenden house in Jericho (fig. 30). Added to the mantel of a small fireplace in

[2] *Ibid.,* figs. 43–46.
[3] Cf. Nancy McClelland, *Historic Wall Papers* (Philadelphia, n.d.) pp. 207–13, for analogous compositions in French papers.

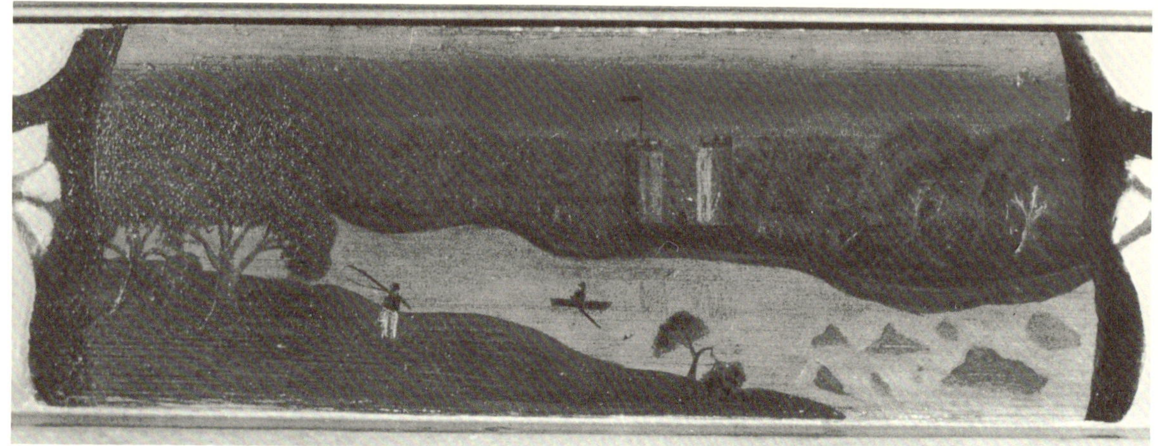

Fig. 30: Painted fireplace mantel in the
Chittenden-Martin House, Jericho, Vermont.

the library at a period considerably later than the great painting in the parlor (fig. 3), it depicts a somewhat less saccharine version of the Weybridge mural. Responding to an age-old human need, the artist has attempted to create castles in Spain for rustics in Vermont.

An old house in East Poultney also contains a large and bizarre mural (66″ x 73″) in the southeast upstairs bedroom (fig. 31). The house was built in 1794 by Deacon Silas How, but the painting appears to have been added some fifty to sixty years later. A flamboyant castle, vaguely reminiscent of Elsinore or perhaps some Flemish manor, forms the principal subject of the mural. There are no visible human occupants. The castle is flanked paradoxically by a tall New England elm. By contrast a decided continental baroque flavor is lent to the work by the presence of a high tower capped by a golden onion dome.

86

The colors are a combination of naturalistic browns, greens, and blues with broad passages of gray employed to indicate a river or bay. An engraving of a European castle, probably altered to disguise its identity, doubtless served as the source of this curious imaginary estate.

An exception to the tendency to embellish one's environment with views of an opulent, far-off life-style is provided by a mural found in an upstairs bedroom of a small farmhouse near London-

FIG. 31: Mural in the Deacon Silas How House,
East Poultney, Vermont.

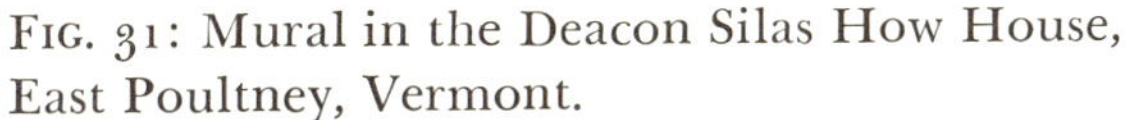

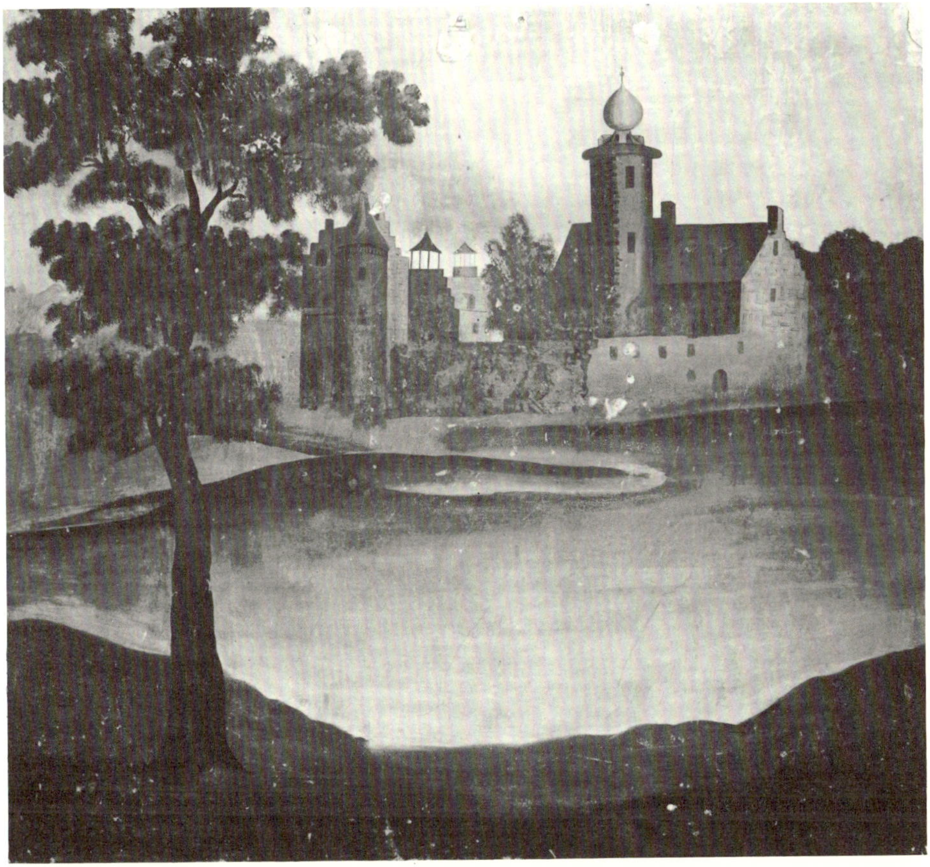

derry (fig. 32).[4] This factual view of a quaint Vermont town stands in marked contrast to the murals discussed previously, though in date it cannot be far removed. A mid-nineteenth-century mural in a house in Fitchburg, Massachusetts, also shows a similar use of parted drapery to achieve a proscenium or stage-like setting.[5]

[4] For the Grant-Taylor house see Herbert W. Congdon, *Old Vermont Houses* (New York, 1946), p. 18 and fig. 14.

[5] Cf. Little, p. 109 and fig. 130, painting by J. H. Warner, 1840. The drapery used as a framing device also appears in a somewhat earlier overmantel in the Palmer house in Canterbury, Connecticut. See Edward B. Allen, *Early American Wall Paintings, 1710–1850* (New Haven, 1926), p. 16 and fig. 15.

FIG. 32: Mural in the Taylor House, Londonderry, Vermont.

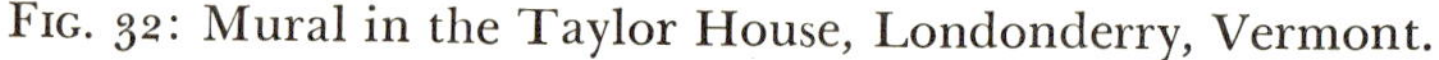

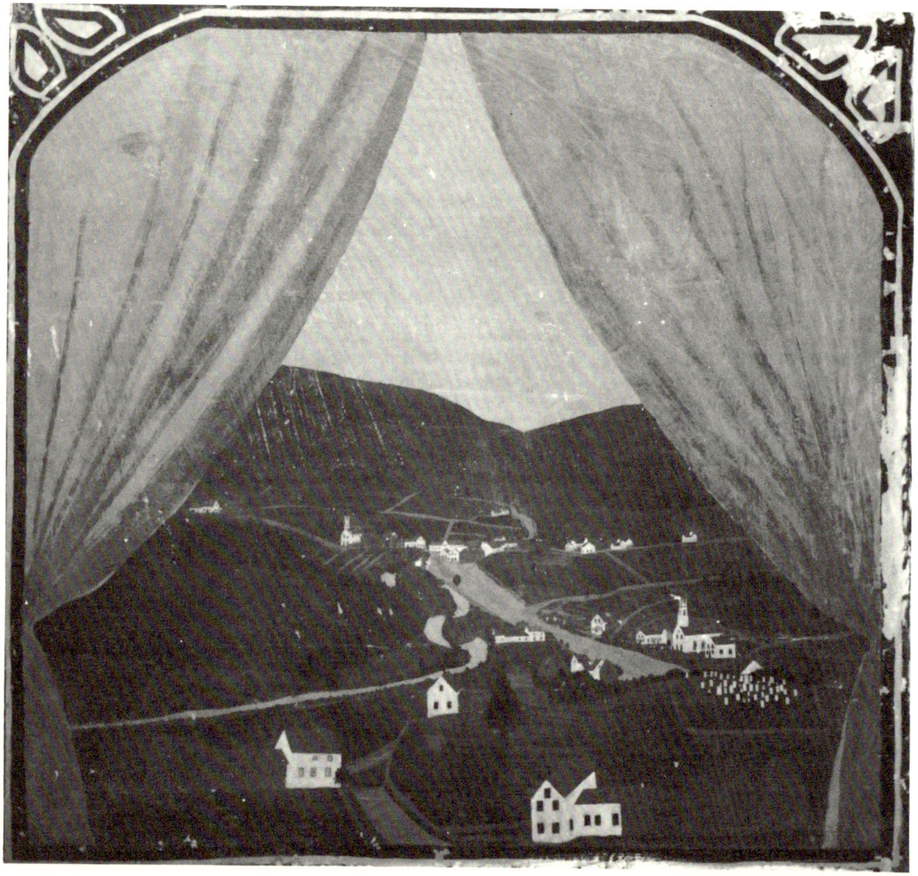

One of the most unusual painted interiors in Vermont was recently discovered beneath several layers of old wallpaper in a rural farmhouse near Clarendon. Although the house dates from about 1800, the decorations were clearly added to the hallway about fifty years later (figs. 33–34). This is indicated by the presence in the corridor of a narrow flu, the surface of which has been decorated with a simulated Corinthian column (fig. 33). Providing visual rather than actual structural support for the ceiling, the column leans perilously inward at a delightful rakish angle.

Around 1850, this type of tall, thin flu was added—as the owners of many colonial homes are sadly aware—to older houses in order to accommodate the recently invented cast-iron stove. Employed as a substitute for the open, drafty colonial fireplace, the iron heating stove achieved widest popularity in New England about the middle of the nineteenth century.

Additional evidence for a midcentury dating of the murals is offered by the forms of the decoration which consist of the luxuriant neoclassical ornament popular at the time. These unique murals, however, were neither derived from wallpapers nor inspired by the native school of wall painters. Instead, the muralist attempted to provide the owner of a Vermont farm house with a painted interior intended to rival a European palace or villa. Unlike the overmantel painters considered earlier, the Clarendon muralist did not seek to suggest through pictorial imagery a more gracious life-style. Rather he strove to attain an effect of elegance by transforming the humble room *in toto* into a palatial setting. That which formerly was illusion has given way to delusion.

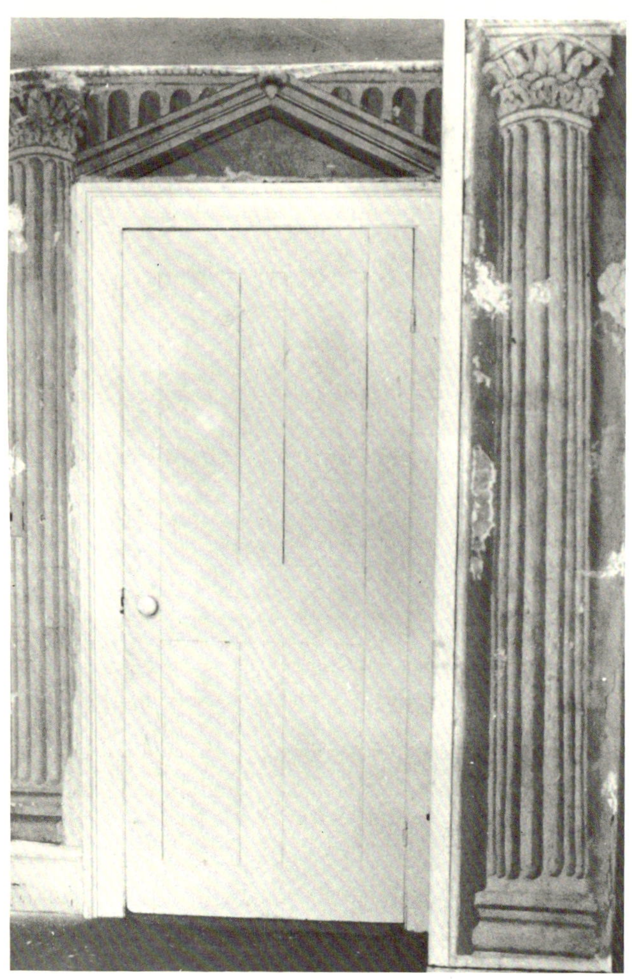

FIG. 33:
Mural in the Howard House,
Clarendon, Vermont.

Although no similar ornament ever existed in any reality other
than the imagination of the decorator, the practice of mixing styles
in architecture generally adheres to the high Victorian preference
for what has aptly been described as "picturesque electicism."[6]
Corinthian columns, neorococo paneling, and ersatz-Victorian

[6] Alan Gowans, *Images of American Living* (New York, 1964), p. 108.

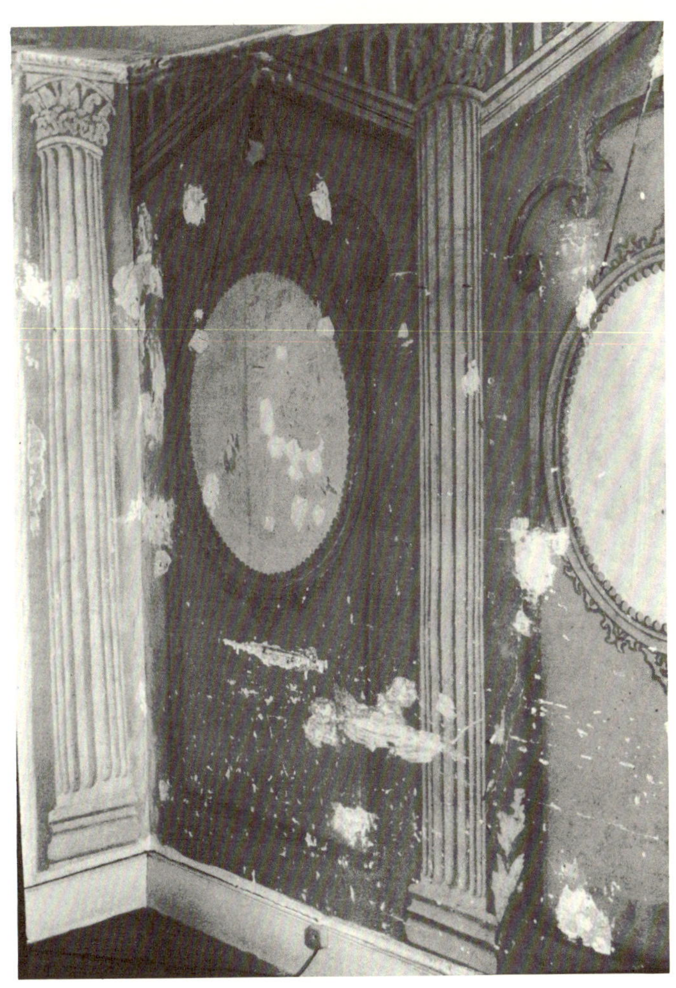

bric-a-brac form a stylistic hybrid that, for all the crudeness of the execution, is not without appeal to an observer sufficiently inured to the taste and affectations of the later nineteenth century. Thus for the modern eye the Clarendon murals are enhanced, paradoxically, by the very qualities of naiveté and rusticity that the muralist aimed to disguise with his painted illusions of grandeur.

In summary most of the above discussed examples of later nineteenth-century wall painting are murals in name only, for they exhibit—apart from their size—few of the formal properties peculiar to that art. In the main, little attempt has been made to adapt them to the architecture of the rooms in which they occur and their appearance is often as much that of a randomly placed easel painting as a mural. An example of the pictorial affinity between these works and other art forms at the time is provided by some painted wire window screens (not shades) (fig. 35) in a charming gothic revival cottage at Strafford. The cottage was built between 1848 and 1851 by Vermont's famous senator Justin Morrill, and the pictures, which are found in the dining room, may be presumed to be of the same period. In subject and treatment they are virtually indistinguishable from several of the previously mentioned murals (Compare figs. 29–31).

The Morrill Cottage, together with its abundant decorations, exhibits a typical Victorian fusion of styles and art forms. In this instance the marriage of the arts is essentially viable as compared to the relative clarity and chaste separation of the arts found in the earlier period.[7] The painted screens, for example, which form

[7] For the Morrill house see Lawrence Wodehouse, "Senator Morrill's Gothic Cottage at Strafford, Vermont," *Antiques,* XCVIII (1970), pp. 237–41. More prominent examples of the Victorian marriage of the arts include the collaboration between Tiffany, La Farge, and Richardson on the Trinity Church at Boston in the 1870s, that between the French sculptor Bartholdi and Richardson on the Brattle Square Church of the same period, and the celebrated collaboration between Sargent, Whistler, and Puvis de Chavannes in the McKim, Mead, and White Boston Public Library of the 1880s. For the career of Richardson see Henry Russell Hitchcock, *The Architecture of H. H. Richardson and His Times* (New York, 1936). On the Boston Public Library see Walter Muir Whitehill, "The Making of an Architectural Masterpiece—The Boston Public Library," *The American Art Journal* II (1970), pp. 13–35.

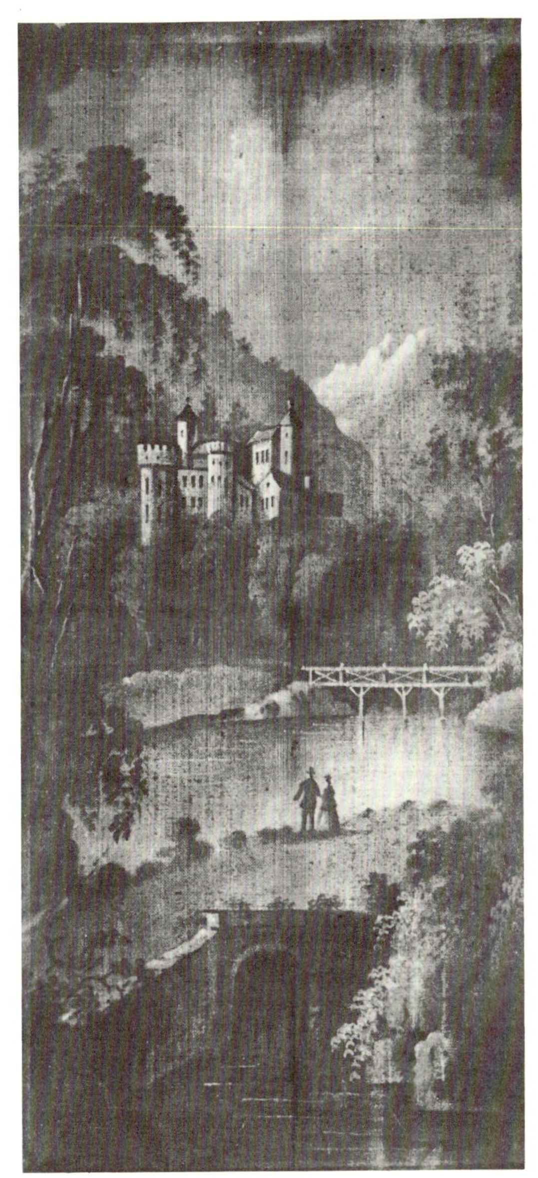

Fig. 35:
Painted window screen
in the Morrill Homestead,
Strafford, Vermont.

charming accessories in the Morrill cottage, would certainly prove inappropriate in a larger Georgian or Federal context. Similarly, a lack of stylistic integration between these romanticizing murals of the period under consideration and the colonial homes to which they have later been added often causes them to appear hopelessly and pathetically misplaced.

2 · Wilson Castle and Shard Villa

The mural decorations of the Howard house in Clarendon (figs. 33–34) mark somewhat belatedly the end of the historic period of early American wall painting in Vermont. There are, to be sure, murals found in Vermont that are later in date, but they elicit images of Borgia popes rather than Yankee farmers. For all the interest that these later paintings provide, they belong more properly to the study of European styles transplanted to America than to the history of the native arts and crafts. In Vermont, one need only view the murals in such mid-Victorian piles as Wilson Castle, near Proctor, or Shard Villa in West Salisbury to appreciate the complex transformation of taste that leads from the simple designs of a Rufus Porter to the bizarre and oppressive pedantries of the later nineteenth century.

On the walls and ceiling of these palaces the pagan gods mix in lurid profusion with the Christian saints while the heroes of antiquity openly cavort with personifications of the arts and letters. Arcadian settings provide the backdrops for recondite events which only the most learned can aspire to decipher. In such circumstances a Rufus Porter could scarcely survive, nor is it likely that he would choose to do so.

One of the finest examples in Vermont of "picturesque eclecticism" in architecture is Wilson Castle. Built by a certain Doctor Johnson, a general practitioner who married well, the castle was finished between the years 1867 and 1874 and filled with heavy furnishings and fashionable curiosities of the era. Not least among the many oddities of the castle are the mural decorations which were completed shortly after 1870 by a minor Bolognese painter, Giuseppe Chiapini, who had been brought over from Italy specifically to undertake the task.[8] According to the little available information on the artist, Chiapini had worked in the Vatican previous to coming to Vermont, and this experience presumably explains his high degree of technical proficiency in the art of mural decoration.

Most of the paintings are executed in the true fresco method, using wet plaster to bind the pigments. This accounts for their superior state of preservation after nearly a century. Chiapini's style is that of an accomplished decorator, skilled in the imitation of classical and Renaissance ornament as well as many of the then fashionable motifs derived from the neoclassical decorations of Percier and Fontaine.

The mural for the hallway ceiling is an especially fine example of Chiapini's decorative skill, simulating an open air loggia similar to those found in many Italian Renaissance palaces. As a device for expanding the space of a room, it is particularly effective and serves to lighten an otherwise thoroughly oppressive interior. The

---

[8] Herbert C. Wilson, the present owner of Wilson Castle, uncovered the facts concerning Dr. Johnson and his muralist Chiapini.

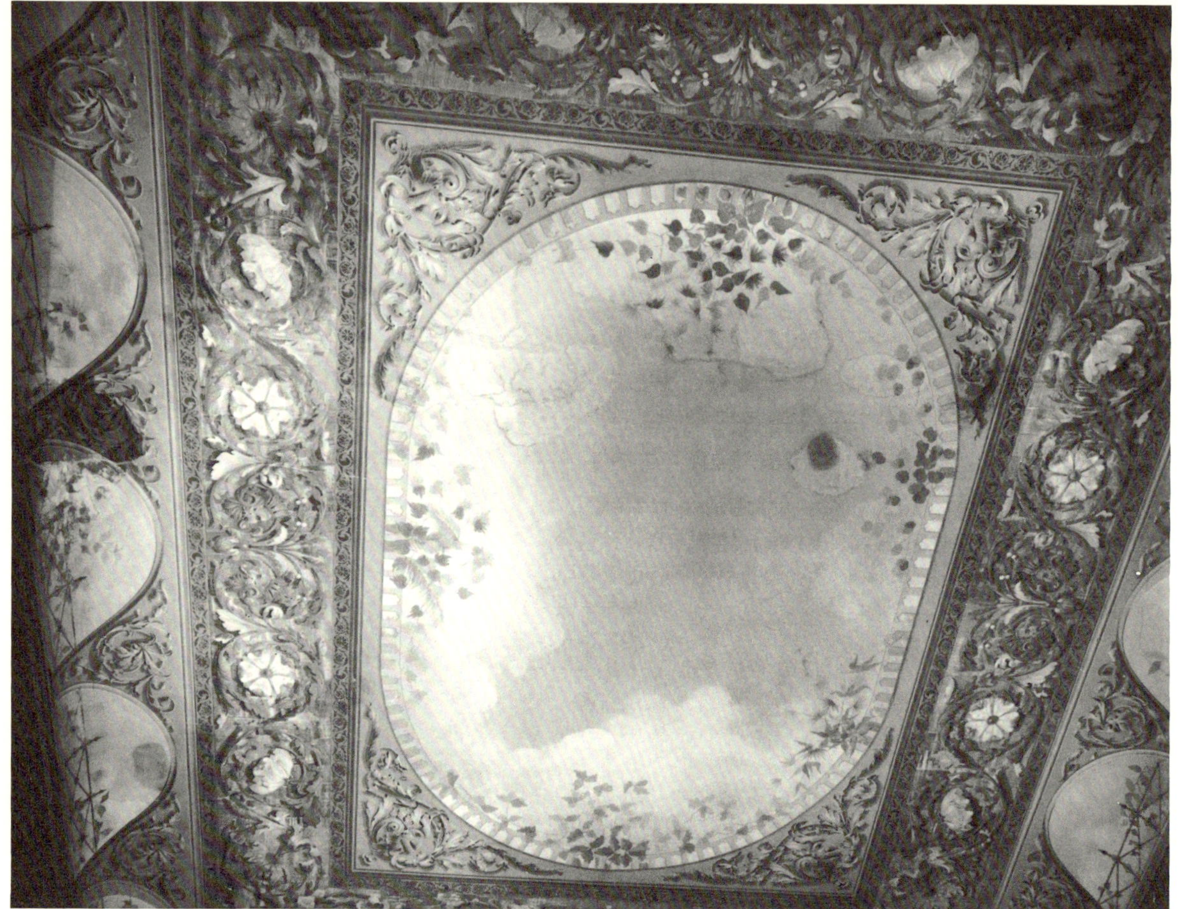

FIG. 36: Ceiling mural in Wilson Castle, Proctor, Vermont.

industrious Chiapini decorated every room in the castle, including the bathrooms, with a seemingly inexhaustible variety of designs.

A house decorated along similar lines also exists in Middletown, Connecticut, dating from about the middle of the nineteenth century.[9] The frescoes in this large mansion are equally accomplished

[9] Allen, p. 101 and figs. 117–27.

and have been attributed to Constantino Brumidi, the so-called American Michelangelo.[10] A Florentine painter who helped to introduce the fashion for Italianate murals into this country, Brumidi was the object of much praise and criticism for his frescoes in the Capitol at Washington. Before coming to this country, Brumidi had worked in the Vatican under Gregory XVI. There he may have made the acquaintance of Chiapini, in which case Brumidi may have been responsible for obtaining the commission which brought his countryman to Vermont. In any case the vogue for Italian muralists seems to have been fairly widespread in New England in the later part of the nineteenth century.

[10] For the unusual career of Brumidi see Myrtle M. Murdock, *Constantino Brumidi, Michelangelo of the United States Capitol* (Washington, D.C., 1950).

F‍IG. 37: Mural in Wilson Castle, Proctor, Vermont.

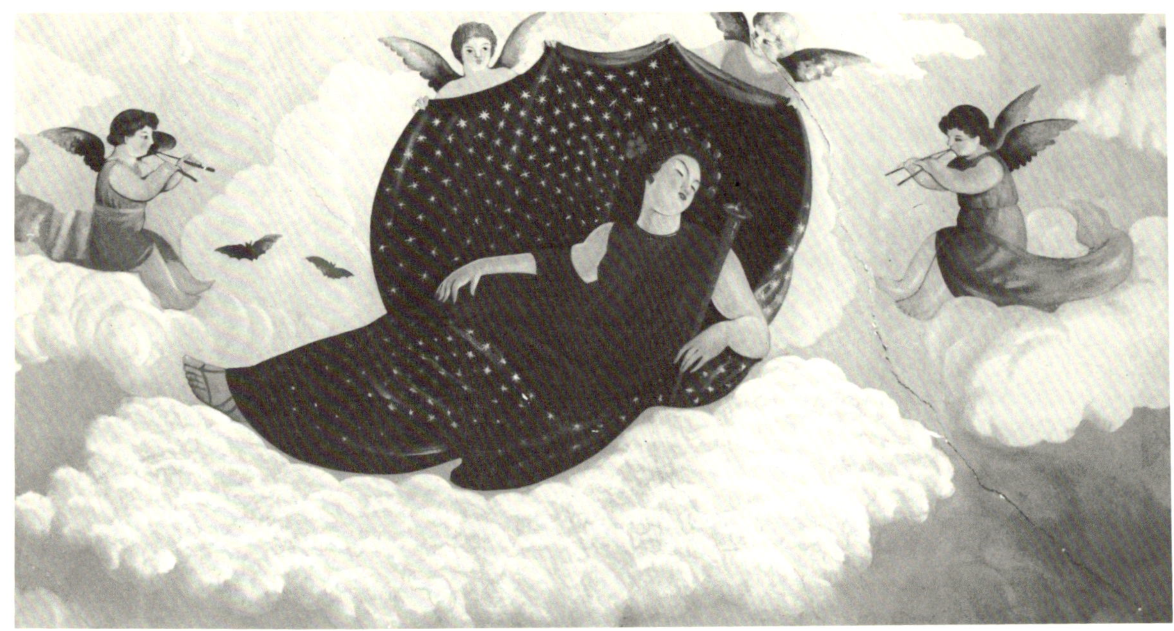

FIG. 38: "La Notte." Ceiling mural in Shard Villa, West Salisbury, Vermont.

By far the most unusual example of Italianate mural decoration found in Vermont—or anywhere else in America for that matter— are the frescoes of the fairytale castle Shard Villa located in the Champlain Valley near the village of West Salisbury. Designed as a dream villa for Columbus Smith, a clever lawyer grown rich on managing claims against intestate European fortunes, Shard Villa was built in the early 1870s during the rage for things "gothick."[11]

[11] For a brief account of Columbus Smith's extraordinary life see Max P. Petersen, "The Yankee Lawyer Who Twisted the Lion's Tail," *Yankee Magazine*, January, 1969. See also Pat Orvis, "Columbus Smith, West Salisbury's Legendary Country Squire," Burlington *Free Press*, July 18, 1964 and J. N. Weeks, *History of Salisbury, Vermont* (Middlebury, Vt., 1860), pp. 322–24.

98

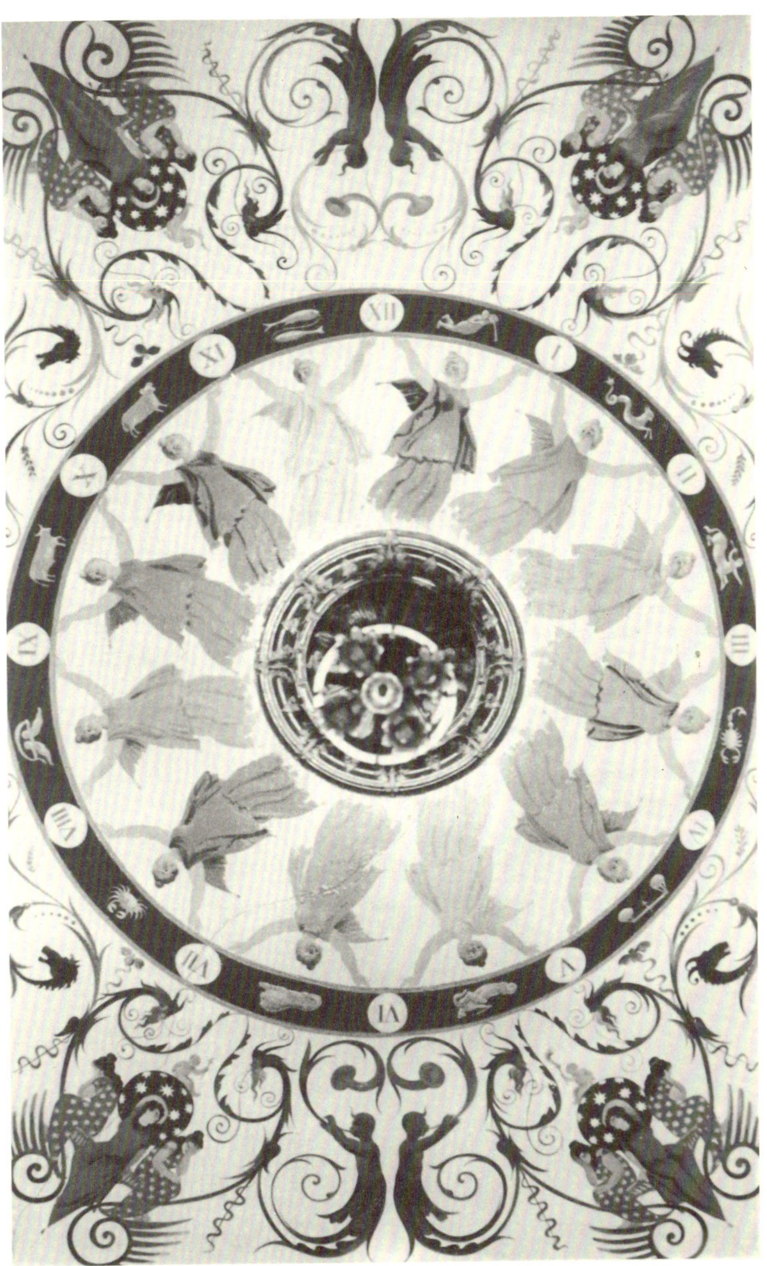

FIG. 39: Ceiling mural in the downstairs hallway
of Shard Villa, West Salisbury, Vermont.

At present a home for aged ladies, the villa still retains many of the original murals in the bright state in which they were painted on the dry plaster. A number of the decorations, however, have fallen victim in recent years to rain damage. Fortunately, one is still able to gain a fairly complete picture of the original scheme of decoration which was as extensive as it was pedantic.

By chance the name of the artist, Sylvio Pezzoli, has also come to light, as have numerous details of his artistic career.[12] Pezzoli was born in Ferrara, Italy, in 1858 and, after studying art in Venice, Florence, and Rome, he came to Vermont in 1886 under commission to decorate Shard Villa for Columbus Smith. The murals, according to a legend, were copied after those in a particular Italian palace with suitable adjustments for their new Vermont setting. In point of fact, however, Pezzoli appears to have devoted considerable skill and attention to developing a mural program especially for his distinguished Yankee patron. The southeast parlor, for instance, is devoted to representations of historic examples of law (e.g., "Socrates Instructing Alcibiades"), in presumed deference to Smith's profession and the source of his wealth (the villa itself was named after his first case).[13] Personifications of Painting and Sculpture in the hallway bear testimony to the lawyer's keen affection for the arts, while a variety of religious scenes in the northeast parlor (copied after such masters as Fra Angelico) reflect his reputed piety. Greek thought, Roman jurisprudence, and Christian morality thus combine to celebrate the wisdom and virtue of the now forgotten Vermont lawyer.

[12] Mr. Sylvie Pezzoli of Garden City, Long Island, a grandson of the painter, was able to furnish me with much of the information regarding his ancestor.

[13] See Petersen.

Pezzoli, whose current fame is even more obscure than his patron's, frescoed other homes in both Vermont and New Hampshire, but no trace of these paintings remains.[14] Later, the painter went to Chicago and Milwaukee where he decorated the homes of many "prominent businessmen." Pezzoli finally settled in Pittsburg where he followed the career of a portrait painter with moderate success.[15]

The murals of Shard Villa, despite their lack of appeal for the modern eye, form a fascinating ensemble dedicated to an interesting man. Today, they bear mute witness to the taste and aspirations of an extraordinary era of the past.

3 · Churches with Painted Decorations

The subject of mural decorations in New England churches and meetinghouses has received only slight attention from students of early American painting.[16] This neglect is understandable since few of these buildings still retain their original painted ornamental interiors. It would be inaccurate to conclude, however, that the practice of decorating churches with some form of simulated

[14] According to Pezzoli's unpublished "Life Memorandum," a copy of which his grandson graciously made available to me, the muralist decorated the house of E. J. Wyer in Salisbury as well as the house of a certain Dr. Sparhock. In New Hampshire Pezzoli worked in the home of a Mr. Farwell, "cashier of the National Bank of Claremont." Inquiries indicate that none of these decorations survive.

[15] *Ibid.*

[16] Little, pp. 113–14, gives a brief account of the subject, observing that "a complete survey of these little Greek Revival buildings from the point of view of painted internal ornament would be a valuable and rewarding study."

architectural ornament was not widespread in New England during the nineteenth century.

The only currently extant example of "deception painting" in a Vermont meetinghouse is found in the Congregational Church in Grafton which was built in 1830 (fig. 40).[17] Painted chiefly in soft greens, browns, and roses, the principal decoration occurs on the end wall of the church. A large semicircular aedicula, partially open to the sky, admits the golden rays of the midday sun. Magically uniting the exterior world with the church interior, the work suggests a visual metaphor for divine or transcendental illumination, though there is little in Congregational theology to support such a notion. More important, so skillful is the spatial illusion that the spectator, upon first entering the church, is amazed to discover that all is painted on the flat plaster wall. Simulated classical moldings and cornices further join the walls to the ceiling on all sides of the interior.

Probably painted in the full flood of the Classic Revival in Vermont, the mural—like the neoclassical ornaments in the Clarendon house—are datable to the middle of the nineteenth century.

Indeed, a possible clue to a closer dating of the Grafton murals is provided by an old photograph of the interior of the First Congregational Church in Gaysville, Vermont, which was built in 1863 and probably decorated at the same time (fig. 41). Painted over in 1964, after more than a century of existence, the Gaysville mural displays similar ornamental details though the effect is heavier, and ultimately far less appealing, than the elegant and fanciful decorations at Grafton.

[17] See R. L. Towne, "What's Happening in Grafton, Vermont?" *Yankee Magazine,* November, 1967.

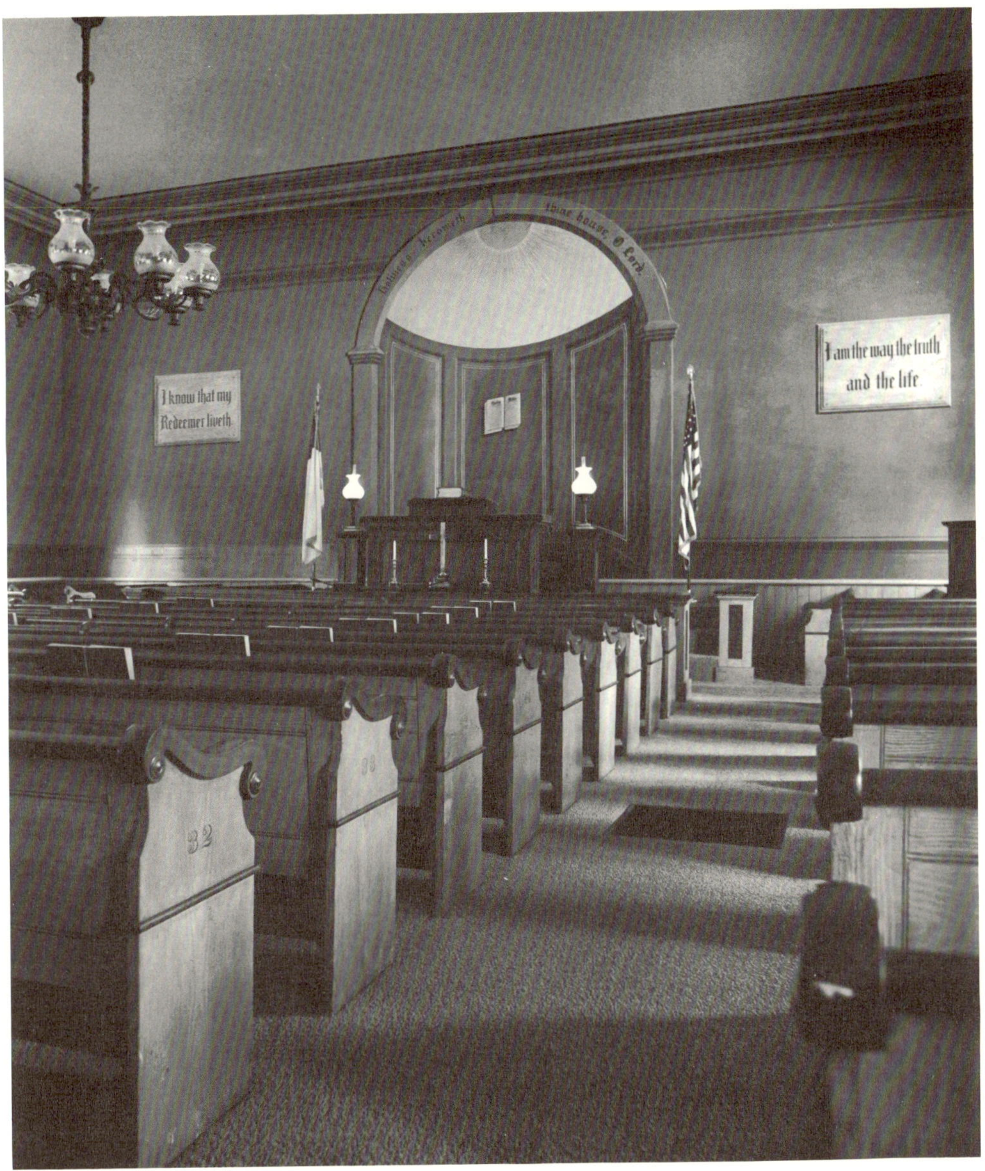

FIG. 40: Mural in the Congregational Church, Grafton,
Vermont. *Photograph courtesy of Yankee Magazine.*

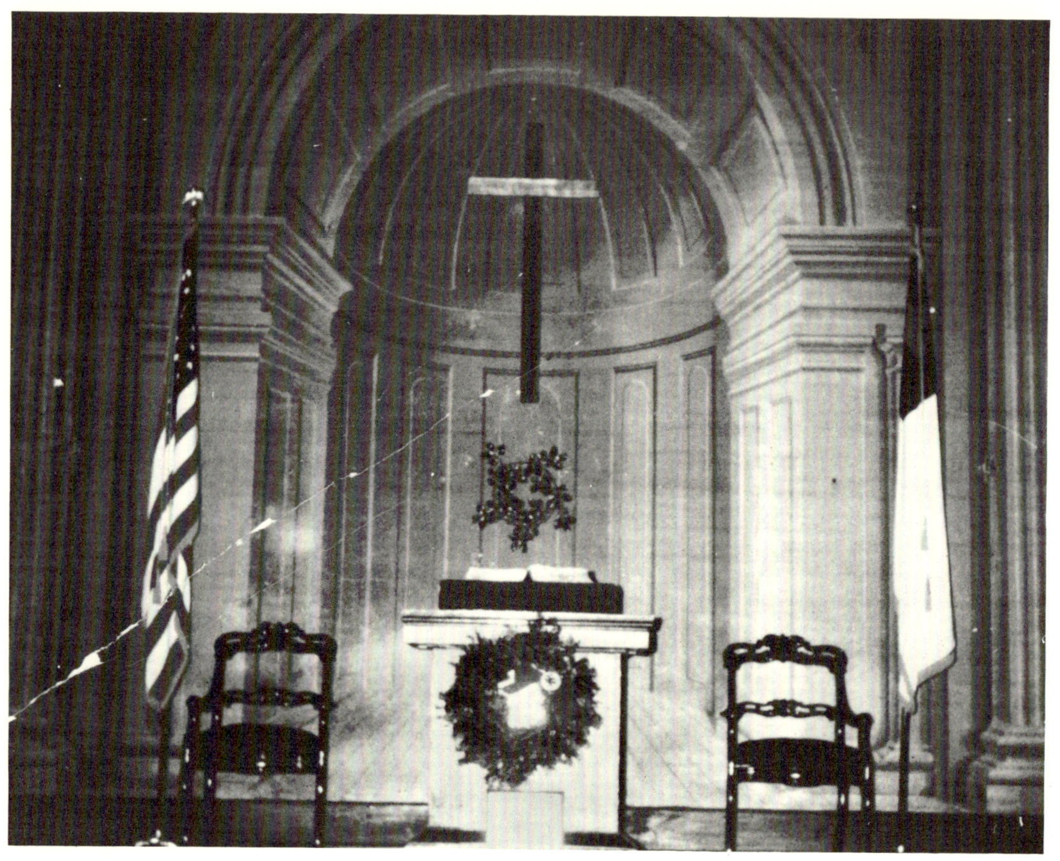

FIG. 41: Photograph of mural (now destroyed) from the
First Congregational Church, Gaysville, Vermont.

In Clarendon, an older member of the Congregational Church
remembers a deception painting on the end wall of the interior
that was painted over "about twenty years ago." And so the story of
destruction continues.

At Bethel, for example, it is not known when the frescoed in-

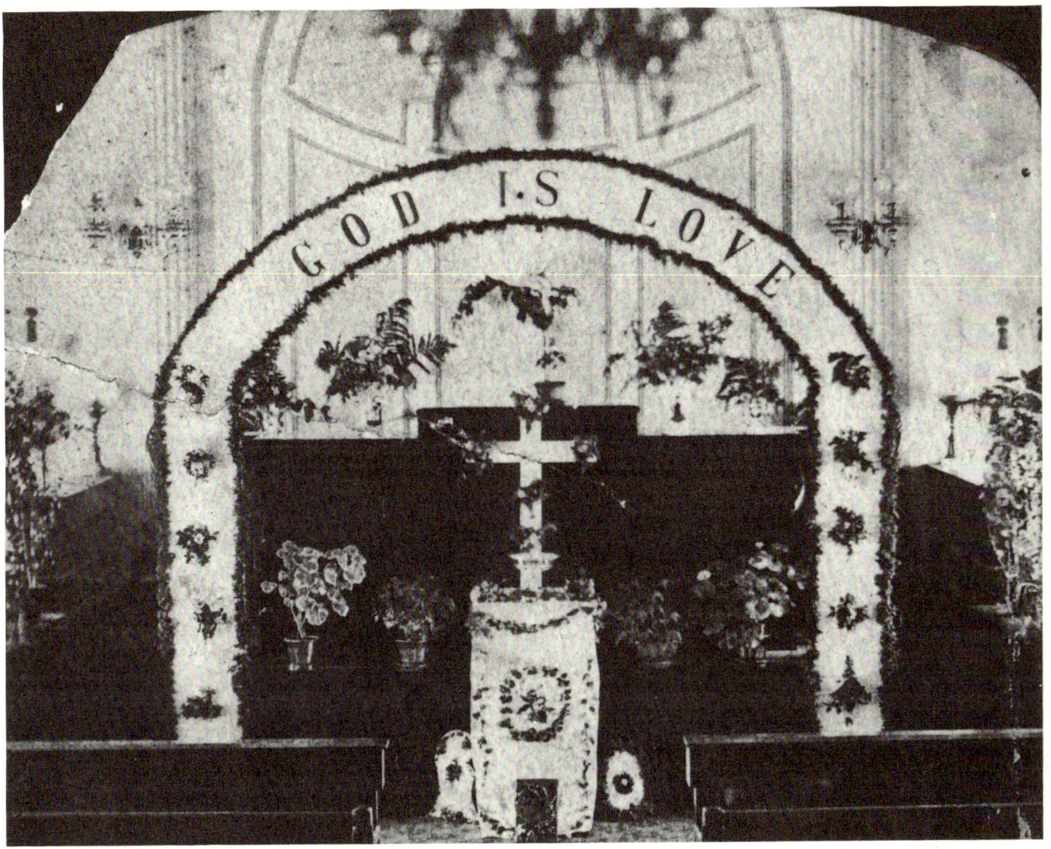

Fig. 42: Photograph of mural (now destroyed) from the United Church, Bethel, Vermont.

terior of the United Church was covered over with a coat of paint. An old photograph taken in 1876 (fig. 42) shows the usual classical hemicycle behind the pulpit, as well as a delightful and topical floral arrangement. It seems likely, therefore, from the above and from evidence that can be adduced from neighboring states that the art of embellishing the interiors of churches with simulated architectural ornament was not an isolated event in Vermont.[18] Most likely the impetus for this development, especially in Vermont and New Hampshire where the majority of examples are found, came from a desire to create a substitute for the more permanent forms of architectural ornament usually found in the meetinghouses of the older and wealthier New England states.

As a final note these church decorations form a modest epilogue to the study of early wall painting in Vermont.

[18] For a decorated church in Head Tide, Maine, see F. C. Brown, "The Congregational Church at Head Tide, Maine," *Old Time New England*, XXX (1940), pp. 95–100. For churches in Hampton Falls and Portsmouth, New Hampshire, see Little, p. 114.